TAZMAMART

ABOUT THE AUTHOR

Aziz BineBine is a Moroccan author and former army officer. Inadvertently involved in the attempted coup d'état of 1971, he spent eighteen years imprisoned at Tazmamart. He now lives in Marrakech.

TAZMAMART

18 Years in Morocco's Secret Prison

AZIZ BINEBINE

Translated by Lulu Norman

This first paperback edition published in 2021

First published in 2020 by
Haus Publishing Ltd
4 Cinnamon Row
London SW11 3TW
www.hauspublishing.com

A CIP catalogue record for this book is available from the British Library

ISBN 978-1-913368-13-5
eISBN 978-1-912208-89-0

Typeset in Garamond by MacGuru Ltd

Printed in the UK by TJ Books

This book has been selected to receive financial assistance from English PEN's PEN Translates programme, supported by Arts Council England. English PEN exists to promote literature and our understanding of it, to uphold writers' freedoms around the world, to campaign against the persecution and imprisonment of writers for stating their views, and to promote the friendly cooperation of writers and the free exchange of ideas. *www.englishpen.org*

To Maman, the woman who brought me into the world
and wept for the ungrateful baby I was,

To Christine, the woman who brought me into the world
the thankful old man I am,

To all those who are grieving the ghosts of Tazmamart,

To you girls, mothers, wives, sisters,

I love you.

Preface

"There are those who cry their pain and those who sing it.
God hears them both, but the song is sweeter to his ears."
– Tagore

I'm a survivor of the years of lead,* a storyteller, a dealer in suffering. I have only my misfortunes to place in your hearts. I am no victim, brothers; save your tears.

This is the song I sing as a former convict.

To come out of prison is to lose all your bearings. Everything has changed: society, the environment, people's mindsets, even family. Some have left, others have arrived. The ex-prisoner falls into this little world like an interloper. What is his role, his place in society, what are his rights and duties? Is a father still a father, faced with children he hasn't seen growing up? How does he contend with the tears of a mother whose heart he's ripped out, or a father whose hopes he's ruined? What can he ask of a wife who's been left to face adversity, deprivation and humiliation alone, often with dependent children?

* The 'years of lead' – generally considered to last from the 1960s to the 1980s – refers to a period of King Hassan II's rule notorious for state violence against dissidents and pro-democracy activists.

And then there's that hell, to paraphrase Sartre: the way other people look at you, the tacit judgment of society, of your friends – old and new – those closest to you, the person you ask for work or for help with paperwork.

Like the newborn separated from the placenta, the freed prisoner must rid himself of the shackles of violence and suffering that have held him for long years. He must learn again to love, to understand, to admit, to forget and also to ignore. Starting again from scratch is never simple or easy, but to do nothing is worse.

Twenty years later, the world had changed. 'The king is dead, long live the king!' A younger, more open, more modern king – but modern with a small 'm', because liberty, democracy and free speech are slow in coming. Which is normal in a society beset by its own demons of traditionalism, passivity and fear. Three decades of dictatorship can't simply be waved away, especially when the palace bastions are still haunted by the temptation to go back to the old ways.

Twenty years later, we were free. Alone, confronting ourselves and other people. Confronting life. We had no idea of values, the values of the society we lived in or the value of feelings, money, possessions – all those tiny things that make up everyday life.

Twenty years later, we were awarded 'compensation' – a sum of money to forget, to forgive, to reconcile ourselves. But with whom? With what? Can you be compensated for your youth, lost in the limbo of prison? For your health, destroyed by disease, cold and vermin? For your mother, whom despair, weakness and disease have carried off?

There is nothing to compensate, nothing to forgive. You must just forget. Ban regret and bitterness from your heart. Live again.

Condemn, you say? Condemn whom? And what? To what end? To get even? Fight fire with fire? An eye for an eye? That's not for me. I would rather be victim than executioner, wound than knife.* Instead of worrying about those who tortured me, my heart overflows with love and gratitude for those generous souls who fought for my freedom, my rights and my humanity. Those righteous souls who turned their lives into a fight for human rights and human dignity.

We had our fairy godmother; her name was Christine Daure-Serfaty. She was the wife of the kingdom's longest-serving political prisoner, Abraham Serfaty, and devoted her life to pleading his cause on the international stage and with various non-governmental agencies. She happened to discover the existence of our prison in the course of her travels, and so her little magic wand began to work its miracles: first by persuading the public that our prison existed, a fact the authorities denied, then by casting a benevolent spell on the writer Gilles Perrault, who wrote a book – *Notre ami le roi* (Our Friend the King) – in which he denounced the appalling conditions of the dungeon where we languished. The spell worked. Forces for good were set in motion to knock down the barricades of *diktat* and injustice. Christine, the fairy godmother, had turned darkness into light.

* A reference to Charles Baudelaire's poem 'L'Héautontimorouménos': "I am the wound and the knife!" ("Je suis la plaie et le couteau!")

Finally, we emerged from our death pit. We left darkness for daylight. We felt the sun's caress on our cheeks, the north wind kissing our foreheads, liberty's sweet embrace. We were broken, ill, distraught, but free. Changed, but free.

But were we? On the outside, certainly; inside we were still inhabited by the spectres of our cells, by the solitude and despair that relentlessly haunted our sleep and our dreams. Never would we be as before. We were doomed to wear the ex-convict's clothes, the insignia of the survivors of hell. Some called us traitors, others called us heroes or saints; in fact we were just poor wretches hung out to dry so that time could do its worst.

Is it possible to halt your destiny for a moment? Ward off the inevitable, lay down your burden? Only for a moment.

Time leads us inexorably towards our fate, leaving in the dust of the universe a trail of blood, tears and prayers.

2019

I dreamed of being a journalist or a filmmaker; I became a soldier. The son and grandson of court officials, I became a revolutionary despite myself. I was a playboy; I became a convict. But as the saying goes, man proposes and God disposes.

My mother was the daughter of an Algerian captain in the French army. He had arrived in Morocco between 1912 and 1915 with the protectorate army that had come to pacify the country, and he was appointed liaison officer working with indigenous peoples – a role that cost him his life. He was poisoned by high-ranking Moroccans afraid that this soldier – French, Arab and a Muslim, just like them – might take their place. He died serving France: a Chevalier de la Légion d'Honneur, he was awarded the Military Medal, the Croix de Guerre, the Medal of Merit and so on. My mother was eight years old and became a ward of the state; at eighteen, she married my father. A musician's son, he was living at the court of El Glaoui,* the famous pasha of Marrakech, and was his most loyal companion.

My father was an *ulema*, one of those learned keepers of faith and religious expertise in an Islamic country where religion and reasoning have always been intertwined and are still

*Thami El Glaoui, pasha of Marrakech 1912–1956, was one of the world's richest men. Hugely powerful in Morocco, he helped the French to overthrow Mohammed V.

great sources of power and wealth, especially when developed under the protective, expansive wing of the 'Prince'.

My father maintained this status quo.

His learning and extensive cultural knowledge had singled him out early to serve the country's greatest men: first El Glaoui and then King Hassan II, to whom he became very close. Having no official duty other than keeping the sovereign company, he would see him day and night, in privileged, intimate moments when the king was at his most relaxed and receptive. Owing to his phenomenal memory and his eloquence, my father had studied literature and Islamic law at the same time. He could quote the finer points of civil or Islamic law, had learned the manuals of Arabic grammar and rhetoric by heart and, as well as Arabic, had perfect command of Berber and French. To cap it all, he had set about memorising all Arabic poetry from the pre-Islamic era onwards. As a young man, he'd been friends with one of the greatest Moroccan poets, Ben Brahim, the 'poet of the Red', who owed this honorific to the colour of his native city, Marrakech. But Ben Brahim could only compose his most beautiful poetry when he was blind drunk. Unfortunately, the morning after, all or part of his creation would have evaporated with the fumes of alcohol. To remedy this, he would ask along my father – who didn't join in the carousing – and the following morning Ben Brahim would come to buy his own poems from him. Having heard them just once, my father had memorised them. When he met my mother, it was love at first sight; he married her, carefully refraining from admitting to the modern young woman that he already had a first wife.

Until the age of sixteen, I was French through my mother. When Algeria gained its independence in 1962, she opted for Moroccan nationality, which was a prerequisite for her application to be a tax inspector. I took my father's nationality as a matter of course; he was Moroccan born and bred, equally at home in Berber and in Arab culture, since his heritage fused the two. When, after taking my baccalaureate, the moment came to choose a career, the easiest solution was to sit the exam for the Royal Military Academy. Since I was part of the very first intake of baccalaureate-holders to this prestigious institution, I became an officer, to my mother's great pride. A pride that would be short-lived, so fate had decreed: a trivial incident, an act of student bravado that in the first instance placed us at the mercy of Colonel Ababou, would alter our lives dramatically, making us protagonists in the darkest act of our country's recent history.

In 1970, at the end of our final year at the academy, we were entitled to some leave, as had been the custom for generations, but for no good reason the director decided to cancel it, sending us instead on an utterly pointless course in mechanics. We considered this a gross injustice and promptly abandoned the course. When we returned the following term, instead of being posted to different army corps – which was what usually happened – our year and the one above were assigned to Colonel Ababou, a man with a reputation for brutality, as a disciplinary measure. We were seconded to Ahermoumou as instructing officers.

Ahermoumou is a small village in the Middle Atlas, huddled at the foot of Jebel Bou Iblan. Winters there are harsh and snowy and the summers extremely hot. The military school was just outside the village on a plateau overlooking an immense sheer cliff, constantly pummelled by the wind. It housed around two thousand cadets as well as the staff and their families. This community sustained the village and was expertly run by Colonel Ababou, assisted by loyal NCOs tasked with managing the barracks. The officers – in this case, us – took care of the teaching.

In Ahermoumou, discipline was iron-fisted – for the cadets as well as for staff, whether they were officers or not. No favouritism was shown, even to those soldiers closest to the colonel. In fact, they were the most fearful of all, since they were in the front line and had more to lose. Not all his men were on a level, however; besides the administrators, a group of henchmen were assigned the dirty work. They were a real mafia, devoted body and soul to their master and led by the infamous warrant officer first-class Akka, who was Ababou's eyes, ears and right hand.

Discipline might have been severe, but the advantages were enormous, and we knew it; when they felt the need, our superiors were only too ready to remind us. Most of us had escaped a nasty punishment, we were put up rent-free in beautiful villas, ate for nothing in the mess and had all the military kit we needed, none of it itemised and with no obligation to return or reimburse it should it be damaged or lost.

Time passed in Ahermoumou as we began to learn about life, about power and responsibility, both in Morocco and within the army. Schoolbooks had taught me that a military career was about 'glory and servitude', when in fact it was glory for the few and servitude for everyone else – if that can be called glory.

We were getting used to authority and discipline. Not everything was black and white; we had to learn the importance of nuance, there being so much of it in our country. Above all, we needed to learn hypocrisy, which was as vital to someone making a career in the army administration as swimming is to a sailor. In this, we had a great master, the grand champion of illusionists and tricksters: Ababou. He'd built a legend around himself in the Royal Armed Forces, according to which he was a kind of Joha* or Ali Baba – a brave-hearted thief at the head of a dedicated commando unit, whose mission it was to scour Fez and the surrounding countryside and seize equipment from communities, businesses or private individuals. Anything that might be lying around and could prove useful for the garrison, or for reinforcing infrastructure on the colonel's farms, was fair game. I wouldn't be surprised if heads of cattle came into it, too. Their audacity was boundless. Unscrupulous men were highly valued at the time; lack of conscience was seen as courage, highway robberies were feats of arms. They were admired, feared and often idolised rather than hated. Attracted to power like flies to honey, these lords grovelled lower than anyone else, the better to bite when the moment came. They knew each other, socialised together and kept a close watch on one another, attempting all the while to conceal their teeth and claws.

The colonel was a short, rather chubby man whose pudgy

* A mischievous joker of popular legend.

face drew attention to his cold, hard stare. He ruled by force, stopping at nothing, and woe betide anyone who stood in his way, because Ababou never forgot a grudge. No doubt it was this resentment that drove him to the insanity of the putsch, which would mean ruin for him and for us. He was furious with the entire world for his having been born small and poor – which was only partly true since the Ababous were an eminent family that had once counted a vizier among them. During the protectorate, the colonel's father was himself a sheik* under the command of Caid Medbouh. Medbouh's son – the famous General Medbouh – would be our man's chief supporter and, more importantly, the mastermind behind his attempted coup. Excel though he might, Ababou would remain Medbouh's subordinate. Every time he stood before the general, decades of stifled resentment stirred within him. His fateful enterprise proved how desperately he dreamed of one day having not just the Medbouhs but many others under his command – and why not be rid of the king himself...? One day, *he* would be lord and master... And he was certainly up to the job. One of the best in his year at the Royal Military Academy, and the very best at the officers' training school, he had succeeded brilliantly in his exams at the École de Guerre in France. This earned him the honour of directing the armed forces' general manoeuvres in Marrakech in 1968, in the presence of King Hassan II himself. During these combat drills, which involved the entire army, each unit had to act according to very precise, predetermined orders so

*Tribal authority, an agent (unconnected to Middle Eastern sheiks).

as to support or fight other units, depending on whether they were acting as allies or enemies. Live ammunition or blanks might be used in these exercises: a formidable trap. Ababou represented the new generation of officers to emerge from that very young Moroccan army, of which he was such a talented member. As the outstanding laureate of the École de Guerre, he was the first officer of that generation to direct manoeuvres on a national scale and perhaps, one day, he would be commander-in-chief of the army. The tiniest blunder could bring his career crashing down. The test was more than conclusive: he received the compliments of the king and the entire military command. That day a new leader was born and with him, perhaps, a lust for power that would jolt the Moroccan political and social system from its torpor.

It was during similar manoeuvres in El Hajeb, not far from the Ahermoumou training school and its Sefrou annex in particular, that Colonel Ababou and General Medbouh's first attempt at a coup was planned to take place. At that time, the Sefrou cadets and their officers were detailed to take part in manoeuvres at El Hajeb, with some reinforcement from us. I was not one of the personnel involved. Everything was ready: the commando unit had been assembled and the infantry were standing by with their vehicles, weapons and ammunition. At the last minute, the order came to break ranks because the school's participation had been called off. We would find out later, after the events at Skhirat, that the king – having caught wind of something, or simply put off by bad weather – had decided against attending. The plan fell through but was only postponed, because, on the morning of 9 July 1971, we received the order to prepare for live firing exercises the next day at Benslimane, a few kilometres from the palace at Skhirat.

We had the whole day to prepare, to assemble our units, do the roll call, check kit and ensure that supplies, weapons and ammunition were correctly distributed. The mission was a delicate one, as the men had no experience of live firing exercises. In fact, they had no experience at all – most of them hadn't been in the army six months. Worse, no officer had command of his own cadets that day.

By evening, everything was ready. The drill had been

rehearsed a few months earlier, but with different actors; this time, the finger of fate pointed to us. After a hard day's work, we gathered for supper in the officers' mess, in combat uniform of course, with guns and ammo. As he entered the mess, the school's doctor, a young French lieutenant doing his military service, exclaimed: "My God, you look like you're planning a coup!" A burst of laughter greeted his remark, but a seed of doubt had been sown.

The next day, every man was at his post. The convoy set off early in the morning. It consisted of twenty or so trucks loaded with men, each led by an officer and an NCO. At the front and back of the convoy were what we referred to as the commandos: light armoured jeeps, some equipped with heavy 12.7mm machine guns and others with anti-tank ammo. There were four soldiers to each jeep, most of them the colonel's men. Later we learned that some of these light units had been given special instructions: to ensure that no soldier or vehicle deviated from the plan. They had orders to shoot anyone who might take it into their head to go walkabout.

The convoy drove the three hundred kilometres from Ahermoumou to Rabat with no difficulty, without once being stopped by gendarmes, police or any kind of roadblock – which in our country is strange to say the least. A few kilometres outside Rabat, near the small town of Sidi Bouknadel, the convoy came to a halt at the edge of a forest. Only the officers had orders to disembark. Ababou was waiting for us with his brother Mohamed, who was older than him but in no way his equal. There were other people, NCOs we'd never seen before. Later we'd find out they were members of his family. He briefed us on the next part of our mission: the unit would divide into two convoys, one under his command and the other under his brother's. Each convoy would go in through one gate, disembark and scatter down the alleys, shooting only on command and preventing anyone from 'coming out'.

But coming out of where?

A crucial point needs making here as regards the location of the action, about which my comrades and I disagreed. Personally, I'd heard the word 'palace'. Some claimed to have heard 'drill grounds' and others agreed with 'palace' but with the understanding that the king was in danger. Where did not the truth but reality lie? Often, time and events distort our memory of the facts.

Destiny had shown her hand; all the players in this drama would be mown down. No one would come out of it unscathed.

The palace at Skhirat was the king's summer residence, where, on his birthday every year, the Festival of Youth was celebrated. Anyone who was anyone in the country's political, diplomatic, military and business worlds would gather around the sovereign on that day. Gendarmes and soldiers from the Royal Guard were on duty at the palace gate. Seeing the convoy, they raised the barrier and stood to attention. We entered, unaware that our orders were entirely fictitious and the king knew nothing of the operation.

We burst onto two avenues which marked the palace boundaries to the north and south. Between them stretched a golf course, a vast expanse of lawn dotted here and there with isolated thickets and a few lone trees, where the king's celebration was taking place: a magnificent, animated cocktail party, a meeting of the country's elite. Behind them stood a long building, a series of state rooms, which at the north end overlooked the royal apartments and their outbuildings. The western façade was punctuated by huge glazed bay windows that overlooked a private beach. The eastern façade, which gave onto the golf course, was completely shuttered. The configuration of the grounds partly accounts for the massacre that took place that day.

The first lesson in fighting that we would give our cadets was that, in the event of ambush, under enemy fire, they must jump out of the truck and return fire. Unhappily, this instruction was applied to the letter.

The convoy led by Ababou's brother entered first, by the northern gate; he arrived facing the golfing green, where the king's many guests were assembled. We were on the other side, preparing to disembark, when we heard a burst of gunfire. Yet no order had been given. Had one of the younger cadets panicked? It remains a mystery. The rout had begun. Following their training, the cadets jumped from the trucks and all of them opened fire. We tried everything to stop them, but it was no use; all we could do was fall flat on our stomachs to avoid stray bullets. A barrage of fire erupted from the two columns of trucks that surrounded the area; it was a two-way massacre. The people still standing on the golf course were mown down in the crossfire, along with many of the cadets. The exact number wasn't revealed after the events, but more than two hundred were felled by their own comrades.

Now it was complete chaos. No one was in charge of anyone, no one knew what to do; Ababou himself had completely lost control of the situation and had been shot in the shoulder the moment he jumped down from the truck. I'd seen cadets fall right in front of me and I couldn't even tell if they were from my unit. I was utterly helpless. I yelled, but it was no use; no one was listening. I wanted to – I should have – called their names, but I didn't know them. By assigning us cadets that weren't our own, they'd limited our ability to act. And it was a disaster.

The shooting stopped; the tumult continued. I stood up to reassemble my unit, but what was left of it? I couldn't say; the list was still in the truck. Which one? Only the driver could have told me, but there was no sign of him, he'd disappeared. Without the list, it was impossible to find men I'd only seen for the first time the night before.

Desperate and disoriented, I decided to walk around to try to assess the situation. There could be no doubt now as to the purpose of the venture I was involved in. It was a horrific sight: bodies lay just about everywhere, drained of their blood. It was the first time I'd seen a dead man up close. The hardest part was coming across the corpse of one of my cadets; I knew that boy, I'd trained him, taught him. He was just a kid. Such a terrible waste.

I entered the palace by a winding corridor and, through a door, immediately found myself in a vast hall that looked onto the beach, with large windows that stopped the wind and sand coming in. The place was empty. Where was the king? Had he taken refuge somewhere? A group of cadets entered at the far end. They saluted automatically, without really noticing me, and went on their way. Where had they come from? Where were they going? Even they didn't know. Suddenly one of them broke away, came up to me and said, "You know, Lieutenant, this glass is bullet-proof. Look!" He fired a round from his sub-machine gun against the window-pane and shook his head. "You see!" Then he went to find his friends, who'd already left.

I was as bereft as they were. I carried on walking, deciding to take the first door I came to. It was unnerving, this abnormally deserted place surrounded by pain, the clamour of death and agonising uncertainty. Outside, bodies were strewn almost everywhere, cadets and civilians alike: rich businessmen, influential politicians and ordinary palace servants, all equal now in death.

Then I found myself next to the golf course, near what looked like the kitchens. Ababou was there, flanked by an NCO and four cadets. He was wandering about like a tortured soul. Pale, his wounded arm at a right angle, he didn't look at me. He seemed lost. I fell into step behind them all when, suddenly, one of the men lying flat on the ground stood up and shouted at him furiously, "Ababou, what the hell's going on?"

A cadet went up to the man and took him by the arm, but he pulled away roughly and went on yelling at the colonel.

"What did we agree?"

Ababou looked at him blankly and replied, almost gently, "Oh, General, is that you? Where's the king?"

"First tell me what you're doing here, at this time. This is not what we agreed!"

General Medbouh clearly did not want to answer the colonel's question; his instinct told him that his protégé had betrayed him. A grain of sand had slipped into the smooth workings of the putsch they had planned together. Medbouh, however, knew that the king was cowering in a back room somewhere, below the state rooms, hiding with General Oufkir and my father, who never left his master's side when the king wasn't performing official duties. Perhaps right now, all three of them were praying no one would think to look behind that concealed door. If he were to reveal the hiding place, Medbouh wasn't sure he could still control the colonel – he sensed the situation had got completely out of hand. He looked at his godson the way a teacher looks at a pupil who's been caught red-handed. Ababou seemed angered more by Medbouh's attitude than by his refusal to disclose the king's hiding place. His strange behaviour showed that he knew the game was up.

Suddenly, he took the general by the arm and led him towards a small thicket, murmuring, "Come, General, we need to talk!"

Turning to the cadets at his side, he motioned them to follow. A shot rang out. A few seconds later, he returned, followed by the cadets but without Medbouh...

At that moment, everyone suspected everyone else, generals betrayed other generals, generals betrayed their king; everyone had forgotten that fate was the final arbiter.

I thanked heaven that I hadn't been caught up in that settling of scores. During my imprisonment, I would often ask myself: had it been me, instead of those cadets, ordered to shoot someone – in this case, the general – what would I have done? Would I have had the courage to refuse and risk being shot myself, or would I have been cowardly enough to carry out the order? God spared me that ordeal. How could I have lived with that weight on my conscience? No, I will not condemn those who had the bad luck to be in the wrong place at the wrong time. May the Lord grant them His pity and their victims His mercy.

I realised how lucky I was and how precarious my position, and decided to get as far away from the colonel as possible, as fast as possible. I had a clear idea now of what had happened: we had taken part in a coup d'état, which apparently had failed. Everything about the colonel's demeanour and the situation on the ground screamed it. I was against it, I was appalled by the way events had unfolded and now, whatever the outcome, "my mind was made up, I would desert", as the song goes.*

I went to the palace car park and looked for a car belonging to a civilian. I happened on a Fiat 600 that had its ignition key on the dashboard. I borrowed it. From that moment on, I was walking a tightrope; on both sides stretched infinite pain.† Whether Ababou succeeded or failed, I was in deep trouble. I needed help. I went to the house of an uncle of mine, who was a police commissioner and close to General Oufkir. He wasn't at home, but I spoke to a cousin who, having listened to my disastrous tale, suggested I go to the house of a friend of hers, who was a Libyan diplomat, to ask his advice. I agreed, clinging to the first lifeline I'd been thrown. The diplomat came to meet us and took control of the situation. He advised me first to leave my uncle's house, because my being there would jeopardise us both. He offered me hospitality, suggesting I stay with him until he could find a way to get me out of the country. No one would or could find me at a diplomat's house, it was true, but here too I faced a moral dilemma: did I have the right to drag people I didn't know down with me? I decided to face up to my responsibility. I asked our friend to take me to the Paratroop

* From 'Le Déserteur', a famous anti-war song written by Boris Vian in 1954. The refrain has since been taken up by other singers to protest many different wars and causes.

† A paraphrase of Corneille's *Le Cid*: "Des deux côtes, mon mal est infini."

Brigade; I would surrender and wait to see what happened next. He dropped me off not far from the barracks, and I presented myself to the guard outside. He alerted the duty officer, who turned out to be the instructor I'd had during my parachute training. The duty officer knew nothing about what had happened and had no idea what to do with me. I outlined the situation and told him I'd come to give myself up. More irritated than anything else, he eventually agreed, took my gun, unloaded it and counted the bullets – something neither the police nor the investigating judge would bother to check. Yet a report had been written; the officer was required to make one. There was no bullet missing from the chamber of my gun.

I wasn't locked up but stayed in the duty office; I was even given some supper. Everyone was on tenterhooks: what was going to happen? Had the putsch succeeded, as the radio declared?

In fact, realising his Skhirat plan was failing – since the king had escaped and the only man who could lead him to the king was dead – the colonel assembled what soldiers he could and headed for the radio station, which was guarded by a former aide of his, Lieutenant Taief, and his unit. Taief tried to bar him from entering and was shot dead on the steps. Once in control of the radio station, they forced a famous Moroccan composer to read a message on air announcing the end of Hassan II's reign and a military takeover. Next, Ababou went to General Staff HQ in Rabat, hoping that all the Royal Moroccan Army units would rally to him. This was his last attempt at a bluff. He'd lost and he knew it: no one followed him. The units had learned that the king was still alive and had received orders to march on Rabat. Those soldiers still at Skhirat who caught wind of these orders and obeyed them were able to extricate themselves, even if they were more or less implicated in the affair; the rest paid with their lives.

Ababou found himself at General Staff HQ, utterly alone. He was soon surrounded by the capital city's armed guard. The cadets under his command gave up without a fight though, in spite of this surrender, some were slaughtered by overzealous officers, whose courage amounted to giving the order to shoot unarmed prisoners. General Bachir, who was then chief of staff, recklessly raced to the head of the unit that had invaded General Staff HQ unopposed. He shouted at the mutineer with these words: "Ababou, you dirty bastard! Give yourself up or I'll kick your arse!"

By way of response, Ababou emptied the rest of his magazine into the body of the elderly general, who also fired and fatally wounded the colonel. Staggering now, Ababou was aware it was all over but refused to give himself up alive. He turned to the faithful Akka and ordered him, "Finish me off!"

Akka had clearly been given precise instructions for this eventuality; he didn't hesitate for a second. He turned the heavy machine gun he held in both hands on his master and fired, before jumping over the wall and vanishing into thin air.

In the middle of the night, the duty captain of the Paratroop Brigade woke me and, sounding slightly embarrassed, asked me to go to the cells, where I was locked up. Destiny had spoken. The next day, I was transferred to the Brigade Légère de la Sécurité where I joined most of my comrades, who were lying on the floor, bound hand and foot. The soldiers of the BLS were clearly not as chivalrous as the paratroopers. I was tied up and thrown among my colleagues like a parcel. We spent the day this way, without food or water. Vengeful soldiers came and booted us in the ribs, thrilled to be able to kick their officers' arses at last. A chance like this was hard to come by.

We had tumbled down all the rungs of the social ladder overnight, but we didn't yet know that our fall was just beginning. In the evening, we were finally untied and all parked – officers, aides, rank and file – in one room; there were a great many cadets, just over a thousand, still alive. The authorities of the day had decided to deal with them separately; they would not be charged, but were instead there as witnesses. It was clear we were already being judged. They wouldn't be looking for who had done what, but for who would take the blame for all of it. Ababou and Medbouh were dead; some of the generals and superior officers, presumed guilty merely for being at Skhirat, had been summarily shot by firing squad the next day. Yet they were only on the golf course as guests of the king, to celebrate the Festival of Youth. Some were accused of planning the coup along with the perpetrators, others of jumping on a moving train. Admittedly, some of the generals had spoken to the colonel at Skhirat, and some of our fellow officers claimed to have seen a few of them at Bouknadel, which implicated them. Personally, I don't believe anyone had come to Bouknadel but that Ababou had attempted to deceive everyone, and the men accused of being with him at the palace or General Staff HQ had been coerced. Were they in on it? I don't know, and I have no desire to rewrite history. But I do know that that day, terror and death were at large. Ababou would stop at nothing, respected nothing and was himself nothing but a wounded beast, dragging everyone down with him.

I'm still convinced that, from the beginning, when I ran into him at Skhirat, Ababou knew that the game was up and had already worked out his exit strategy. But he wasn't the type to go quietly. He'd decided to fight to the last, settle his scores and wreak as much devastation as possible. And here we were, penned like cattle in that room in the BLS that was too small to hold us all; we couldn't lie down, or even go out to relieve ourselves. A two-hundred-litre barrel was set up in the middle of the room for a toilet. You had to have someone else's help to climb up it and the lights stayed on day and night so, as a further humiliation, we had to expose ourselves. This was real torture for the shyest among us, who also suffered the taunting of the soldiers, overjoyed to find the boot on the other foot, so to speak. I realised I needed to swallow my pride and make myself as small as possible, try to pass unnoticed, bend so as not to break. Days went by, heavy with bitterness and disillusionment; it was one humiliation after another. We were being initiated into misery and degradation. Our own friends from the academy, if they weren't insulting us, came to jeer; we were traitors, outcasts, unbelievers.

After three weeks, we were transferred – cuffed and blindfolded – to the Sûreté Nationale, the national police headquarters. The interrogations lasted a fortnight; not once were our blindfolds or handcuffs removed. The food was good, the police officers polite. Later we learned that General Oufkir was monitoring the judicial procedure himself. He'd given express orders that we should not be roughed up. He'd also insisted the interrogations be conducted by police officers, which wasn't mandatory in our case; everything relating to the army lies within the jurisdiction of the gendarmerie. Some will put this down to their alleged involvement in the coup d'état, but I don't believe that. Having himself been the director of the SN, Oufkir favoured an organisation he was familiar with and could handle, where he still had some influence. I'd like to believe there was a modicum of military solidarity in this. What hurt me the most about this whole sorry adventure, afterwards and still today, was the position the army took towards us. Unlike the parties, organisations and opposition movements that were and remained supportive of members who fell foul of the authorities during the years of lead, the army treated us as lepers. The political class would reject us, projecting all its hatred and fear of the military onto us, and the army would deny us, in an attempt to cover up its own sins.

At the end of the interrogations, they made us sign a blank

sheet of paper and sent us to Kenitra military penitentiary to await trial. In Kenitra, we came under the command of the gendarmes and Commandant Bouazza, formerly of the colonial army. From the rank and file, Bouazza had fought his way to the top using his fists and especially by his habit of recklessly charging over battlefields, where men like him served as cannon fodder for the French. He retained a certain clumsiness from his past, and a coarse but direct manner of speech. In any case, he did not suffer fools and had no qualms about showing the big shots in security that inside the prison, he was boss. Bouazza was one of the few military men to show us any compassion and never hesitated to tell anyone who would listen that we were victims, that it was a shame to lose so many young officers. I still have fond memories of that blunt but humane old man, at a time when the least gesture of sympathy meant so much. The commandant showed his worth in particular the day he obtained permission for us to be seen by a doctor. This was utterly miraculous; a few of us were even admitted to hospital.

There was an occasion when I put him to the test. It was during the time when, one by one, we were allowed to go out to the yard to get some air, though we still had no rights. A fellow prisoner offered me some warm underwear. I accepted. This was the wrong move, because instantly I began to itch all over. Suspecting something, I used my walk in the yard to make sure: the underwear in question was swarming with lice and had infested the rest of my clothes. There was no way I could live with those revolting creatures. I wasn't ashamed to shout loudly for Commandant Bouazza, the only one who might listen to me and would surely understand. I made such a racket that eventually he was informed. He came to see me, and I explained the situation. Without answering, he turned to his aide and ordered him to bring me some DDT powder. I sprinkled it all over my clothes, my body and my cell. Two days later, I had a good shower. The scourge had been eradicated. That incident rid me of lice but uncovered quite a few fellow sufferers who, from modesty or shame, were stoically letting themselves be devoured.

At long last it was the trial. We were inordinately naive, sincerely believing we had no need of lawyers: we were innocent, and the process would be a mere formality. We did not know that, in a speech, the king had referred to the famous theory of 'rational obedience', according to which a subordinate is never compelled to obey an unlawful order. That simple phrase had condemned us in advance. We had no idea either that the monarch had decided we would be judged not by a military court, as the law required, but by a special tribunal presided over by a civilian with the assistance of senior officers. Defence was provided either by officially appointed lawyers or those engaged by some of the accused – mostly Ababou's relatives – and by volunteers, some of whom were there purely to promote themselves. Others, who were scarce but much better prepared, had come for moral or ideological reasons. I won't dwell on the stance taken by the leader of the Istiqlal Party, Mr Allal al-Fassi, who asked the party's lawyers not to undertake our defence. His reaction may be chalked up to a political position that he alone will have to justify before history's tribunal but, as for those who obeyed him, what excuse do they have for failing in their primary duty: to defend?

My court-appointed lawyer, whose name I won't disclose out of charity, made an appearance right at the start of the trial, even bringing me a packet of cigarettes. He posed for the TV cameras and disappeared until the day of the verdict, which would be broadcast live. So I appeared with no support.

My case began badly: the day of my hearing, the presiding judge was very aggressive towards me. Either he didn't like the look of me or he had a bone to pick with someone in my family – my father perhaps, since he visited the palace from time to time. My file stated that I knew the palace premises well, which was untrue, and that I was tasked by the colonel to look for the king at Skhirat, which was even more untrue and based on nothing, neither proof nor confession. The day we were to plead, the presiding judge assigned a young lawyer to represent me. She happened to be at the tribunal by some chance or other and improvised a speech that would have been far better suited to a local fundraiser.

I was sentenced to ten years in prison, on purely circumstantial evidence. The curtain had fallen on my illusions, if I had any left; the reality was harsh, but I had to accept it. A new life was beginning. I had ten years in prison ahead of me, and the sooner I assumed my new role, the better it would be for me.

Life in the penitentiary went on, though less rigidly than before. Once we'd been judged and sentenced, we were allowed visits and could receive post and parcels from our families. It was the usual daily round of prison life: eating, sleeping, a little exercise and reading. When I'd been transferred to Kenitra, I'd begun to pray along with everyone else. Up until then, I'd pray automatically five times a day, and from time to time read some passages from the Qur'an. I considered myself a Muslim, but I wasn't inclined to practise much. From a very young age, I'd gone over the principal belief systems, beginning with Brahmanism and Buddhism. I'd read the Vedas, the Gita and Confucius, studied the Old and New Testaments. In common with my fellow Muslims, I had more or less accurate notions of Islam, and that was it.

Like anyone who's suffering, in a state of uncertainty or profoundly affected by the vagaries of life, I sought refuge in a self-interested faith and began to pray fervently before the trial. The trade-off was clear: Lord, set me free and I will adore You. I had never asked myself what I had done for the Lord or His creatures, what I had made of my own self or my life. When the verdict came down, so did my faltering young faith: I stopped praying, without a fight, without blame and without the least compunction. I felt like an outsider, Meursault at his mother's funeral.

Then, one day, it happened. I couldn't say where it came from or how. There was no angel, no white light; I heard no voices.

I was walking with my fellow prisoners along the corridor of our cell block, on our way to the yard for our daily walk, when I turned to them and cried out, “I surrender unconditionally!”

They stared at me in amazement. They didn’t understand, must have thought I was losing my mind. No one was surprised anymore by other people’s bizarre behaviour after everything we’d been through; it was normality that was off its rocker.

I turned around again, went back to my cell, took some clean clothes and made my way to the washbasins to do my ritual ablutions, partial and full, and say the daily prayers. I had surrendered to God unconditionally, without a second thought and with no other motive than the salvation of my soul. I promised never to ask for anything in exchange and I kept this promise to the end. I was committing to a challenge, an ultimate test that would give meaning to my life. Everything that was happening to me and that was yet to happen fitted into what to me was a logical order of things. This, from my point of view, was the whole meaning of the word ‘Islam’.

Through this challenge, I discovered two essential things: God and myself. I’d surrendered to God, I’d capitulated without asking for anything in return. To give without expectation, without hypocrisy, to give for everything I’d received, for everything I’d taken and undertaken, simply to give. Throughout my long ordeal, I performed my religious duty without ever doubting, without blaming heaven, without ever confusing my faith with my fate. I was there by the will of men; I would leave by the grace of God. If I’d departed from this rule for even an instant, I would have been lost.

A few weeks after the verdict, some police units arrived unexpectedly and transferred us from the military penitentiary to Kenitra's main prison. From that moment on, we were treated as civilians and could consequently expect political prisoner status. And so it was. The prison administration accorded us a certain respect. We were exempt from the chores and hard work that the rest of the inmates were assigned. We were entitled to receive supplies, books and radios; we had the right to exercise and play football. We were, at that time, the prison's favoured few.

The infirmary was open to us and we made the most of it. The doctors were happy to write prescriptions for every kind of tranquilliser and antidepressant, following the principle that every prisoner is a potential patient.

One day, I was in the infirmary when they brought in a civilian prisoner who was obviously faking illness. Looking him up and down, the nurse turned to the doctor and said, "This one's not ill, Doctor, he's play-acting!"

"The fact of being a prisoner is an illness in itself, my friend. This man is ill, and we must treat him as such."

Proust said, "Like lovers when they fall in love, like poets when they sing, the ill are closer to their souls." Prisoners, too, are closer to theirs.

Inside, we mixed with civilian inmates. As soon as they crossed the threshold of our block to do the cleaning, their hostility vanished. The muscular disparities that define prison hierarchies began to soften, and their features relaxed. In short, they regained their dignity.

Why this change, simply by going through a barrier? Was it

the sense of security? No doubt. Finding themselves in a more rational environment, they were seeking – even for the duration of the chore – proof that even prisoners can retain their humanity. We were the living example: we had escaped material contingencies through ideals and principles, faith and culture. They were impressed, too, by the number of books they saw in our cells. Knowledge can be intimidating to the uneducated.

When people live in doubt, uncertainty and ignorance, they indulge in all kinds of speculation. From the start of this disastrous adventure, rumours were rife. What extraordinary misinformation circulated after the second coup attempt against Hassan II, the 'air coup' of 1972. A group of pilots (officers and NCOs) had intercepted the Boeing 727 that was bringing the king back from France and attempted to force it to land at their airbase in Kenitra. Several times they'd tried to shoot it down. Though damaged, the royal plane managed to land at Rabat airport. By some miracle, the king was unharmed. The mutineers attacked the palace and bombarded the buildings, but army units overran the airbase and arrested everyone there. Accused of being behind the failed coup, General Oufkir was executed the same day. What fantastical stories did the rounds about those behind the new putsch attempt, about the king's *baraka*, the different talismans he always carried on him, the gri-gris fashioned by powerful *fqihs* in league with Shamharoush, king of the djinns. He had a whole arsenal of supernatural protection, as infallible as the amulet Pasha El Glaoui had given him before he died, the famous 'Tbarides' which apparently rendered him invulnerable to bullets. In this jumble of rumours, one passed almost unnoticed. It concerned a military prison being built in the desert. Its name was Tazmamart.

The rebel pilots replaced us at Kenitra military penitentiary and, after their trial, they were transferred to the main prison, like us; by now, the circuit was well-oiled. Due to lack of space, they were put in the wing reserved for those condemned to death. Was this a sign from fate? After the release of those of us who had lighter sentences, say eighteen months, there was more room. Then, in the middle of the night, the pilots were transferred to the available cells. We could hardly wait for morning to meet them and were already thinking about the best way to approach them. Now we were all together, pilots and infantrymen. We hoped for the best; it would be for the worst.

We did not meet – and never would meet – our new neighbours, except by voice, because at the dead of night, in the heavy heat of August 1973, hordes of police officers and gendarmes swarmed the building, opened our cells one by one, blindfolded and cuffed us and loaded us into trucks parked in the prison yard. Even during the coup itself, I'd never seen a deployment of force on this scale. They must have planned it carefully; the operation didn't take long. In no time at all, the cells were emptied and we were on our way. The trucks took the road to the airbase where army planes were on standby. We landed at dawn – we had no idea where, and in any case couldn't see: it was Rachidia airport. Other trucks, military ones this time, awaited us. We set off into the unknown.

When the vehicles came to a standstill, I heard a sound

that was already familiar, of cell doors being locked: two short clacks, followed by a resounding echo, like a gong at the bottom of a well or a cave. When my turn came, two hands grabbed me by the shoulders and stood me upright. I tottered forwards down the truck. As soon as I was close to the edge, I was shoved into the void. In that moment, I was winded, my mind a complete blur; I could hardly feel my body. It must have been a symptom of panic. As I fell, four solid arms gripped me and stood me on ground that felt very soft. I hadn't yet recovered when I found myself facing what from now on would be my tomb: cell number thirteen.

My cave was a shadowy concrete cube, two metres by three; even the dim light of day barely impinged on the darkness. At the back was a block of concrete by way of a bench. In the corner, near the door, was a squat toilet. Three rows of holes, each ten centimetres in diameter, had been bored into the top of the wall next to the corridor. In the centre of the ceiling, a similar-sized hole allowed air to circulate. Above that was some kind of hangar, about 180 metres high, which formed a level above the cells. That level, which we could barely make out, had a corrugated iron roof and openings at each end, crisscrossed with bars. The cell doors lined a central corridor that ran the length of the block. A steel-clad vent in the middle of the corridor's ceiling was our only indirect source of air and light.

This was my new abode. I'd never been superstitious, at least not about dates and numbers, but, like everyone struck by misfortune, I began to be.

As soon as the door was shut, I was in the dark. A heavy silence hung over the block. Even the birds had stopped chirping. The sound of soldiers' boots and the abrupt clack of locks and doors made no impression on the emptiness that engulfed my mind and soul. I looked into this pit without really believing it. It made me think of the Christians' cave in the Bible. The idea made me smile. As if death had a religion!

I took stock of my situation. "What have you done, oh you

I see…"* I was standing in what appeared to be my grave. Number thirteen: it was the worst cell of all. The squat toilets had no U-bend – the stench of the sewers from both blocks in the prison came through them – and the smell was so bad that every time the guards opened the door to give me my ration, they recoiled, buffeted by fetid air. The roof had holes like Gruyère cheese, and every time it rained, the cell turned into a shower. When it stopped raining outside, it carried on in my cell for at least another week, the time it took for the puddle on the roof to drain away. In winter, when the temperature fell below zero, it became unbearable.

The only furnishings were the block of concrete and two army blankets that dated from 1936, now worn threadbare. On the floor was a plastic water pitcher shaped like an amphora that could hold about five litres, and a small plastic carafe and plate.

I had to take action, and fast; I needed to make some radical decisions. First, I had to eradicate any questioning from my mind, rid it of anything that might hamper, paralyse or drag it downwards, into the chasms of doubt and despair.

When I heard the locks snap shut, echoing like gongs, I realised we were going to be here for some time. So I decided I must forget the world outside. I no longer had a family,

* From Paul Verlaine's prison poem, 'Le ciel est par-dessus le toit', written in 1880. This line comes from the last stanza, in which Verlaine is addressing himself in prison: "What have you done, oh you I see here, / endlessly weeping, / tell me, what have you done / with your youth?" ("Qu'as-tu fait, ô toi que voilà / Pleurant sans cesse, / Dis, qu'as-tu fait, toi que voilà, / De ta jeunesse?")

or friends. I had no personal memories and no future. I was here and here only. My cell was my universe; my companions in misfortune my only society; culture and faith my only wealth. I had to completely resign myself, to forget the whys and wherefores and accept what I called my three sentences.

The sentence imposed by men, by whose will I was here, which I decided not to appeal because, albeit unwittingly, I had entered a man's home with a weapon, I had violated his personal space and the peace of his family and children. In our culture, we say: "It's entirely lawful for someone who breaks into your house to die" – entirely legitimate, I would say.

Next, the sentence imposed by heaven, which I accepted unconditionally as a challenge, a trial, a cross to bear: my own. For me, life is an ultimate test. There are some to whom God gives everything and some from whom He takes everything. He observes how each person reacts. I am still convinced that, had He given me everything, I would have foundered; today I would be a pot-bellied old general, alcoholic and utterly corrupt.

And lastly, my own sentence: since I was responsible for my destiny, I could only plead guilty. I was both Sisyphus and Antigone, resigned and courageous. After this trial on three charges, my ego had been neutralised and the question 'why' nullified; now I could live and survive, fully embrace the present and alone decide my fate.

Outside, the sounds of the soldiers stopped abruptly and all we could hear was the purr of the trucks' engines fading into the distance, carrying with them whatever uncertainty remained as to our fate. The day passed slowly and the silence became even more oppressive; time seemed to have stopped, life was suspended. Even the birds stayed obstinately mute, their silence heavy with premonition. Then a timid voice called out, carried by its echo across cold, blank walls, as if seeking a gap or refuge in the reinforced concrete. Another followed, then another. Questions were coming from all sides, with answers no one heard, strange names, distorted voices, and that pitiless concrete which, like a vampire grown ravenous after years of famine, greedily sucked up these scraps of life. The birds, surprised at nature's stubbornness and men's optimistic fatalism, overcame their doubts and joined the general commotion at last.

At midday the guards arrived. They served us a small bread roll and a carafe of chickpeas boiled in water with a little salt. This would be Tazmamart's eternal, unchanging menu, with a pot of pasta for supper, again boiled in slightly salty water.

As the transfer had taken place in mid-August, we each received a khaki canvas shirt and trousers, the classic military summer uniform. The striped uniforms of civilian prison were taken away, though we kept the plastic sandals we'd arrived wearing. We swapped our clothes quite cheerfully. Deep down, we were almost relieved to take off that shameful apparel in favour of the more or less reputable uniform of the army, to which – after all – we still belonged. Despite the horror of our surroundings, it imparted the semblance of respectability. Of all we had lost – which was everything – the hardest to bear was the loss of our dignity. That illusion of regaining respectability by being restored to a military body did not last long. We'd taken a step back only to leap further into the abyss.

From the beginning of October, the temperature began to drop. After summer's suffocating heat, we would encounter the torments of glacial winters in pre-Saharan lands, combined with the bitter climate of the Middle Atlas. Autumn was very short and temperatures plunged ever downwards. We begged for a winter uniform, as was customary in the army, but it was no use. We came up against what would be our daily lot from now on: indifference.

*

In order to sleep at night, I would fold my blanket width-wise to make a band of about ten inches. That way I had something thick to wedge between my ribs and hips and the concrete because, of course, I could only lie on my side. If I wanted to turn over, I had to get up, repeat the operation and lie back down again on the other side having rearranged everything, in other words, having put the other blanket – also folded in two – over me, so I could carefully tuck the edges under my body. The secret lay in not leaving even the tiniest opening for the cold to get in. Every time my body shifted, I had to perform a complicated gymnastic manoeuvre, like a never-ending ritual. The smallest crack in my improvised shell became an instrument of torture, a stake piercing my skin and bone continuously; the overall temperature inside the shelter instantly became unbearable. To put it right, I had to start all over again. Having said that, time didn't matter. As the days went on, I became more adept and my adjustments less frequent. That allowed me to sleep more and wear myself out a little less.

Once I was under the blanket, every movement entailed a risk. So I had to put up with the pain in my hip and my shoulders for as long as I possibly could and, above all, save the stored-up air, not allowing any to escape except at the point when I could not breathe. Any heat source was worth saving; nothing must be lost. I would hold in the tiniest little fart – with all the starch we swallowed every day, God knows there were enough of them – until I was under the blanket and certain it wouldn't be wasted. Smell? What smell? There were so many of them. More every day. We didn't even notice them any more. We'd made the stench seem ordinary, as we had the hunger, the cold and all the rest of it – thirst too, since the water we were given was polluted. When we poured it into the plastic pot, the sides immediately turned viscous and a film of sludge settled in it. We decided early on not to drink it. Since the food was liquid for the most part, it was unlikely we would die of thirst. So we didn't drink this filthy water unless we absolutely had to. Those who departed from this rule paid for it with their lives.

In winter, we had to walk. From the corner near the door to the one between the toilet and the bed was the diagonal of life, the walking diagonal. There was only one: four steps one way and four the other, a half-turn to left and right alternately, so as not to get dizzy. I'd learned that at the cinema. When I wasn't walking, I was praying; it was good physical exercise. I'd decided to pay off the debts I owed to God. In Islam, prayer is encouraged from the age of twelve, so I decided to pray not five but thirty-five times a day, which gave me an extra six days and was a good way to keep myself going.

In the first days, we got to know our direct neighbours. We fell into two distinct groups, aviation and infantry, and each group was divided in two: ex-officers and ex-NCOs. Managing the groups was one of the first priorities of our new life, and so I made friends with Lieutenant Ben Chemsi, my first contact among the pilots. We both realised the importance of breaking down barriers, to ease the atmosphere as quickly as possible and root out not just animosity and distrust on both sides but the need to mark one's territory, acoustically and psychologically.

Luckily, everyone understood that the sooner differences were levelled, the better off we'd be. We agreed on a timetable: after the evening prayer, no one would speak until the guards arrived in the morning, unless of course there was a burning need. During the day, in our half of the block, we would speak in turn. At first, there were a few bottlenecks, some friction here and there, but nothing too serious. If someone was speaking, the others listened. For us sailors shipwrecked on an ocean of silence, it was vital to latch on to any sonic flotsam that washed up against the concrete blocks, which would be swallowed by the holes in the walls to feed our hopes and dreams. In our darkness, hearing became the chief sense by which we clung to life. And this was how my being in that cave found its purpose: I became a merchant of dreams, a master of the imagination, a magician of the voice and an impromptu storyteller. This was my contribution to the life of the group: voyaging by voice. I wasn't there for nothing, then…

It had all begun when I was twelve. I can still see myself on my bike, pedalling towards the lycée. I was in the first year of secondary school and every day I'd pass the town hall of the Marrakech medina, an imposing building that was modern for the time. I found its architecture both beautiful and intriguing: it contained all the ambiguity of our culture in its mixture of servile modernity linked with colonisation and traditionalism with all its constraints. I only knew the building's exterior. One day, having left school early, I decided to explore. Large, well-kept gardens surrounded the premises. I walked around it and found myself in a car park facing a door as large and majestic as the one at the front. To the right of the building, a staircase led down to a door half-hidden by plants, above which – placed there like an invitation – was a sign bearing the magic word: Library.

I was captivated. I knew that a library was a public place, I knew it was the home of knowledge and culture – I had been educated in a school of the French Republic – but I was intimidated and went away. That evening, and every evening afterwards, that sign haunted me. Finally one day I took my courage in both hands and made my way to Ali Baba's cave. I entered a vast room, not particularly clean, where silence and darkness held sway. Laden with knowledge and dreams, rows of shelves crisscrossed the room and all of them seemed to be turned towards an old man with a bushy moustache who sat at a desk on a raised platform near the door, like a class supervisor. I walked up to him shyly, awed as much by the place as by its guardian. The cultural heritage of colonialism spread before my eyes; all my youthful past was there and, I'd find out later, part of my future – the part that would give birth to the impromptu storyteller.

On one shelf, a name caught my attention. It had a resonance at once mysterious, nostalgic and poetic: Henri Troyat. I took down the book and read the title, which aroused my curiosity: *La Neige en deuil.** I approached the old man and, trying to sound confident, said, "I'll take this one."

"Do you have a card, young man?"

Of course: you had to be a member, have a card and pay a subscription. I had none of that.

The old man gave me a long, hard look; he must have read all the distress and disappointment in my eyes at that moment.

"Well," he said, "I'm going to trust you. I'll give you the book, but you have to bring it back when you've finished it. And if you want to go on reading, bring me a copy of your birth certificate, a photograph and the membership fee."

I left almost at a run and that same night, in my room, by candlelight – for fear my mother would see my light on and make me go to sleep – I read the entire book. I'd just caught reading fever and soon I would go off and devour the whole of Marrakech Municipal Library. I never had a card, I never paid a fee and I never stole any books; I loved them too much,

* *La Neige en deuil* (translated as *The Snow in Mourning*) is a 1952 novel by Henri Troyat (1911–2007). It was later made into a film, *The Mountain*, with Spencer Tracy.

and under no circumstances would I betray the trust of the angel Gabriel.

In the depths of my cell, that period of my childhood caught up with me. I became a storyteller. I didn't dislike the role – it gave me immense pleasure – although the effort of remembering was considerable. Every night, I would journey into the past. I'd dust off my old books, go back to those popular neighbourhood cinemas, summon the warm, engaging voice of my nanny who used to fill my evenings with amazing stories and legends. Then, in the morning, I would deliver my nightly haul to prisoners who, hanging on my every word, would drink in my voice, making the most of this foray, this window opened onto dreaming, and, for some, onto a whole new culture: the French literary past, the great Russian authors of the nineteenth century and the Americans of the early twentieth.

This went on for years. Sometimes, to give me a rest, one of my comrades would take up the baton to tell a story, but I was indisputably the star the entire prison block would wait to hear. One day, a comrade sent me a bit of bread. This was cataclysmic: I couldn't get over it, a starving man sharing his meagre fare. It was simply a way of showing his gratitude. After thanking him, I had to choke back sobs. I had just received the supreme blessing – the Goncourt, the Nobel Prize – this was the reward for my pains. Deep in my cell, in the dirt, the cold, the despair and the horror, I had planted a tree, the most beautiful of trees, and now it was bearing fruit: learning and dreams trumped the cruelty of men. After this, other comrades sent me crusts of bread, in other words their most precious possession.

In the beginning these sessions were confined to our side of the block, but very soon the other side joined us and the journey became a collective one.

As time went on, the well began to run dry. After using up all the stories I could remember, I started picking up scraps of stories eroded by time. Then I called on my imagination and, night after night, would occupy myself putting together jigsaw puzzles, inventing the missing pieces. Sometimes I'd join up fragments of different stories, other times I made them up and, in the end, after rummaging through every drawer, I turned myself into an author. I began to narrate my own stories. At first I didn't tell anyone, but when they met with success I finally owned up to the deception.

Stories are dreams, writing is action, and the whole paradoxical art of the storyteller lies in this subtle blend of indolence and will.

Besides storytelling, I found myself another vocation: timekeeper. I began to keep a calendar, starting on the day we had arrived. I recorded the Gregorian and Hijri dates and updated it every day. With the help of the guards, I paid attention to leap years and adjusted the lunar calendar. All of it mentally, of course. Then, aided by the birds, the far-off cry of the muezzin and other random noises, I tackled the clock. I managed to work out the time, give or take a few minutes, which kept me busy and allowed me to feel useful. Capturing time like this was also a way to escape it. I'd become time's vessel. The more it passed, the more I counted the days, hours, minutes; the more it passed, the more I counted and kept counting. Then the numbers lost their consistency and dissolved into eternity.

Another way to escape boredom was mental arithmetic. I liked working out sums in my head. First, adding with just one number, then two, then three and so on. When I thought I had mastered adding, I progressed to multiplication. I spent hours doing and redoing the same sums. I looked for tricks to make them easier and reduce the number of errors. When I felt ready, I asked my neighbours for help – with the exception of my neighbour to the right, Captain Bendourou, formerly my direct superior officer and my nemesis at Tazmamart. I would take a number with several figures and multiply it by another number; each of my fellow prisoners would multiply the first number by just one figure from the second, then we'd add up their respective results and theoretically the sum would turn out the same as my own. In the beginning, I made a lot of mistakes but, with time, I improved and thus kept my brain active – at least for the first ten or twelve years because, towards the end, the lack of oxygen got the better of my neurones.

I liked another sort of arithmetic: counting the raindrops when it rained. The roof leaked everywhere; every time, the cell would be flooded. A corner of the concrete block was the only place I could take shelter, bent double, my knees drawn up to my chin, wrapped up in my blankets, which were scant protection from the splashes. I'd sometimes spend a week like this, glued to my corner, motionless, frozen, paralysed, my only activity counting the raindrops, attempting to calculate the quantity of water pouring into the cell. Over one day, I'd reach dizzying amounts before losing myself in the maze of numbers and volumes. I'd give up for a while, the better to start again later; I counted to stop myself going mad.

In the worst moments, as in the better – because even in hell there are better moments, otherwise suffering would have no meaning – I was never far from my memory, my imagination, my calculations, nor, of course, from my soul. I was like a tree with its roots planted in faith and its uppermost branches reaching into culture and the imagination. Through dreams I could breathe, whether it was day or night. Abundant dreams protected our sleep from discomfort, cold, hunger and anguish. To dream was to sleep, to recover, to escape.

My first dream at Tazmamart made a strong impression on me. I've never been able to forget it. I've had some extraordinary dreams, but that one is as clear to me today as it was that first night. I was in the vast courtyard of the riad I grew up in, with its central fountain surrounded by four flowerbeds and overshadowed by fruit trees, which kept the patio – and my memories – fresh. In the corner opposite the bedrooms was the kitchen, whose simplicity contrasted with the luxury of the other rooms. It was a square room with walls that, despite a layer of whitewash, retained the traces of the days spent cooking over a wood fire. At the back of this kitchen, a narrow door led to a corner that was known as the well room. There was a slightly raised well in it, which my mother had had covered for fear that one of us children would fall into it. This well was a great help before we had running water. The rest of the room, which was used to store junk, was long and thin. It was always dark, with a faint smell of damp.

In the dream, I saw myself in the space next to the well, digging. When the hole was quite deep, I lay down in it and started covering myself with earth. It was the strangest sensation; I was both dead man and gravedigger, and I experienced the sensations of each of them: I could feel the wood of the shovel in my palms, the weight of the shovelful, I could hear the sound of the earth on top of me. It weighed on my body, got into my clothes and filled my eyes, my mouth, my ears. Then I woke up. I opened my eyes, looked around me, at the cell, the air holes, the dismal grey walls, the vaporous silence that pervaded the block. I was calm; I wasn't afraid. This wasn't a nightmare. I never told anyone in Tazmamart this dream. I kept it to myself. I was convinced it had a meaning that I couldn't understand, that I wouldn't try to. That day I had the intuition that I would come out of this hole alive.

This swirl of dreams carried on until the last day. All the past I'd banished from my memory came back insidiously to haunt my sleep.

Tazmamart was most of all about men. Living and dead, angels and demons, wise men and mad men – men, just men, flung into a world where horror and extremes had become commonplace. I want to pay homage to those men, the ones who are not here to tell their suffering, their joy, their hopes and regrets. I want to relate as honestly as possible how they lived and how they died, report it as I lived it, as I felt it, for their families and for everyone who feels on their own cheek the slap that someone else receives.

Among these men, in the cell opposite mine, was Driss Dghoughi – a strange fate for someone born with the name Kacem. His father was an old man whose first wife had borne him many children; the eldest, whose name was Driss, was forty years old at the time our hero was born. The old woman, no longer of childbearing age, urged her husband to take a young village girl as a second wife, whom she herself would choose and to whom she would propose marriage on his behalf. "She will have the children," she told him, "and I will bring them up."

And so it was. Our friend Kacem came into the world swaddled in the love of two women. Very quickly the stepmother asserted her rights over the child who, as time went on, became her own son. And woe betide anyone who claimed otherwise! Young Kacem, very naturally, called her 'Mama' and his biological mother by her first name. Fate gave irony a further twist: when the child reached school age, his 'mother' demanded he be educated and not remain illiterate like his older brothers. For this, the family needed civil status. His father took charge and registered all his children at the town hall at the same time, but inadvertently mixed up Kacem's and Driss's dates of birth. When the child went to request a birth certificate so he could be enrolled at school, they were surprised to discover he was forty-five years of age and therefore too old. To correct this error, a judicial ruling would be necessary, as well as a series of complicated procedures.

The simplest solution appeared to be for the two brothers to swap first names. So, at the age of five, Kacem became Driss. He inherited his half-brother's name, just as he'd already inherited his mother, and so was able to go to school.

He joined the air force and went to the USA to complete his training. He had gone off to be a pilot, and everything seemed to be going well for him: he could take off, fly and navigate very well. But he was no good at landing. So he was failed and sent back to air traffic control.

Dghoughi remained inconsolable, struck by the curse of Icarus and condemned to the agony of Tantalus. He was helping others do what he'd never been able to manage himself: to land. He drowned his frustration in alcohol, gambling and women; anything, in fact, that might help him forget his failure. His life was oddly regimented: he would work for twenty-four hours – during which he was sober and focused on his work, which he carried out conscientiously – and then he would spend his forty-eight hours off drunk out of his skull or in the arms of a prostitute. Eventually he happened on a prostitute who fell for him and moved in with him for good.

She'd found a home, albeit temporarily, a man she believed was hers and an illusory dignity. It suited him too: she cooked his meals, did his laundry and the washing up, mopped the floor and even drank with him, without ever asking anything in return. Since he spent all his pay on gambling and alcohol, he never wondered where the food and household extras were coming from. This went on for some years until the day his mother – his stepmother – decided to put some order into his life. She came looking for him and persuaded him to take as his wife a sweet young village girl she had chosen for him. He agreed and, in his immense naivety, thought it quite natural to discuss this with his current companion. She took the news like a stab in the back, but made no comment and even suggested staying with him until his marriage.

Patiently and steadily, she planned her revenge. First, she went to consult all the old medicine women who hovered around the prostitutes' world – *her* world – and, from the panoply of poisons and venoms they'd concocted, chose one that would ruin her lover's health for good but would not kill him. Then she asked around among the other girls, looking for a man said to have late-stage syphilis. She went to see him, slept with him until she felt sure she'd been infected, then came back to the traitor and passed it on to him. At last she had her revenge.

On the fatal day, forever sullied, doomed as surely as he was, she packed her bags and, thinking of her rival, said in a calm voice that was almost free of resentment: "Goodbye. I bequeath her all the misery of my condition."

Nevertheless, Driss Kacem Dghoughi, faithless lover,

blessed child of his stepmother-mother, was married. He gained a secure and lawful union, but lost his health forever. He suffered excruciating migraines and had no appetite – or, when he did eat, could keep nothing down. Syphilitic in the extreme, he wasn't able to father children.

His wife, a village girl brought up to respect tradition – which is a disguised form of the fear of men – accepted her martyr's fate with downcast eyes. Dghoughi, for his part, drowned himself in industrial quantities of alcohol and antidepressants. He became a regular at the military hospitals' psychiatric departments. But medicine could do nothing for him. He was incurable, plague-ridden, desperate, living only to assuage his pain.

Then came the attempted coup. By that time, he'd been off sick for months, and he had only just gone back to work when this new curse struck. He spent his first year of detention in the prison infirmary, where the doctor administered Valium shots to calm him. But then, the fatal blow: he was transferred to Tazmamart. He had the cell opposite mine, and everyone who knew him predicted that his neighbours wouldn't have a moment's peace. Nothing of the sort; Driss clung to life, and to me. We talked a great deal. He would speak and I would listen, no matter what time it was. In the early days, those comrades who were aware of his condition allowed him to talk at night, so he would call out to me and we'd drive out his demons together. I had to convince him that his obsessions were generated by his body, which was in withdrawal from the drugs. He had to admit and accept this; he had no choice. In Tazmamart, no one had any choice. The only possible attitude was mental resistance. We had to hold on to our dignity to the end, no matter what. That was the one thing no one could take from us. Driss survived Tazmamart. When the African prisoners arrived, he was transferred to Block 1, where he managed to get by. When he came out, he was examined by a doctor, underwent tests – and no longer had syphilis!

Today, he's gone back to his wife, who waited for him. He no longer needs medication but still cannot have children.

Dghoughi remains my greatest source of pride from my time in Tazmamart. If only for him, I cannot regret having been there, and I have no qualms about admitting it.

Living in isolation, we would all help each other; we'd either be coming out together, or staying there together.

Of my closest neighbours, only the one to my right did not share this view. He'd decided to go it alone and lived in hatred and resentment, making his own life hell. His name was Bendourou, and I will come to him towards the end. On my left was Sergeant Abdelaziz Ababou, a butterfly who'd singed his wings by flying into the light of his illustrious elders. Opposite him, next to Dghoughi, was Achour, a character straight out of Dostoevsky's worst imaginings.

This was the human environment I was confronted with; to me it reflected all the meanderings of the Moroccan soul and showed me my own image. Through contact with my near and distant neighbours, I learned to recognise and distinguish the important from the futile, the lasting from the incidental. I learned to go beyond anger and hatred, to try to understand, to forgive; I won't say to love. Love attracts and frightens me at the same time. I learned about love by studying the Gospel, in my encounter with Jesus. I'm a confirmed Muslim who loves Christ. I reject some of Christianity's dogma, but I admire its prophet because he taught me what it means to love my neighbour, to forgive and to be humble.

My whirling dreams often featured prophets, probably because we were learning the Qur'an, which mentions them all. After Jesus, my favourite was Moses. He would appear in my dreams, and we'd have long conversations. To me he represented strength, majesty and justice. That, at least, is the way the Holy Book describes him. Each of them inspired different feelings in me. For Moses, it was friendship. I also saw Abraham, Joseph, David, Solomon and many others. And Muhammad brought me freedom in my faith and an unmediated practice.

One night in particular, I had a dream that marked me, which I kept to myself as I did other dreams and thoughts that I wished to remain private. I had a secret garden, a corner of myself that was for me alone. I saw myself lying on my concrete block in my usual position when I abruptly awoke (still in the dream). At my feet stood a tall man in white robes who stared at me, looking at me with the kindest expression; I stared at him too, in silence, for a long time, wondering at the light radiating from him, then I lay down again, utterly serene, and went back to sleep.

The next day, I thought it had been a vision. I had seen Christ in person. And yet I don't believe in miracles. Still today, I'm convinced it was a dream, but one that did me a lot of good: the miracle of autosuggestion. I never saw the prophet Muhammad, perhaps because some teachers of the faith have forbidden his visual representation. Those prohibitions are so sacred, so deeply rooted in our unconscious that we don't dare disobey them, even in our dreams.

Dreams brought us comfort and peace; after all, what did these prophets – their religions, beliefs or ideals – matter? What mattered to us was what they represented: love, kindness, justice, goodness, beauty. In my mind, religion was so simple. There it was – beyond dogma and beyond men, who made it so complicated and so absurd.

Religion helped me overcome the madness and death that constantly shadowed my illusions and my naivety. It wasn't long before they knocked at our door, carrying off someone I'd just had time to get to know and like. They cut down Benchemssi, known as Chmicha, which means 'little sun' in Arabic. We hadn't known him long, since he was the first to go. He was a peaceable, self-possessed boy who had a certain influence over his friends. This had been very useful to us in the beginning, to ease the tension between the two groups, the pilots and the infantry from Skhirat.

Up until his last breath, Chmicha could never understand or accept what was happening to him, the fact that he was in this hole. He couldn't see why his life, the career he was so proud of, the social position he'd fought so hard for, why all of it had disappeared in a puff of smoke – just like the smoke from the shells that, ripping through the cabin of the royal plane, had blown up not only the lives and families of dozens of the army's rank and file, but the apathy of society, the army and our country's regime.

It was particularly hard for him to accept that he would never again see the mother who had such a special place in his heart and to whom, I think, he owed everything. He lost his mind, stopped eating and covering himself. He spent long hours sitting on the ground, in the cold and solitude of his insanity, next to his poor mother, whom he saw up close in the half-light of his purgatory. He'd either lie down on his side, resting his weary head on his mother's lap, the way children do in front of the fire before going to sleep, or he'd sit facing her, feeding her, comforting her, begging her not to be sad. "I'm here, Mama, don't cry," he would say. "I'm coming, here, have something to eat. I'm coming Mama, I won't be long, please don't cry, forgive me, Mama!"

Then he'd disappear into the labyrinth of his ill mind, which was heavy with lethargy and regrets, and turn up again later in our auditory universe, still chasing his beloved ghost and still deaf to our pleas and our anguish.

When the guards arrived, they'd find food scattered all over the floor and him naked, with no blankets over him, in the glacial winter cold. Frozen to the marrow, his limbs too stiff to move, he was soon unable to get to the door to retrieve his food. Since the guards refused to take it to him, it stayed there until the following meal. Then they'd throw out the untouched food and, without washing the pot, refill it and leave it by the door. Chmicha was somewhere else. He went on talking to his mother, oblivious to everything around him. It all happened very quickly: he died on 22 February 1974, six months to the day after we'd arrived.

Realising at breakfast that he was dead, the guards didn't appear all morning. At midday, when they left us our rations, they brought a stretcher and took him away. We were bewildered but, once the shock had sunk in, the commentary started up. Some said he was dead and the guards had taken him off to bury him, and others wanted to believe they were taking him to hospital to treat him. The block was divided on this point for a long time, and it only became clear a year later, after the second death, which was Kinat's.

Then came the first Ramadan. We were hoping for some improvement in our daily lives – wasn't this the month of believers, after all? Apparently not; some people believe only when and how it suits them. The food didn't change one bit, only the mealtimes were altered: when we broke our fast, we were given the daily bread with coffee juice, the boiled starch, a bowl of pasta and our water ration. Then we were locked in for twenty-four hours straight and each had to occupy ourselves. I decided to eat my meal in one go and tighten my belt until the next day. The first Ramadan was difficult, but later we got used to it. We learned how to manage food, and especially time, because in this permanent darkness we couldn't tell day from night. The doors were opened only once a day, instead of the usual three. To cap it all, some of the guards advised us not to fast, since religion exempts us from fasting in unfavourable conditions. Of course they were 'unfavourable', but what were we going to do? Was this cynicism or naivety on their part? More likely just stupidity.

In the early years, when I still had the strength, I decided to fast for two months in a row. In Islam, we can impose this penance on ourselves when we've committed certain sins. I wanted to prolong the fast as a form of contrition but also to test myself. It was tough, very tough, but I managed it a first time and repeated it a few years later. That was the last time. My body no longer obeyed me. Still, fasting remained a therapy. I listened to my body. At the least sign of trouble – slight diarrhoea, say, the urge to vomit, in fact any problem relating to the digestive tract – I would stop eating for twenty-four or forty-eight hours. Sometimes, when the guards were in a better mood, I'd ask them to bring me some sprigs of rosemary or thyme, plants that grew in their barracks' yard. I would dry them, rub them between my palms for a long time and swallow them with water in little gulps. Those were the only remedies available to me, but they were effective, just as much as raising our spirits using our imagination, the fabulous, the fantastical, superstition or the magic potion concocted by Kinat, our soothsayer at Tazmamart.

Kinat was the interpreter of dreams, the purveyor of hope. Every morning we had our news round: each of us related his dream and everyone listened to the interpretation in case it contained some auspicious sign. As soon as we closed our eyes, we began to dream. I felt as if all I did in my sleep was dream, there were always so many to report. Although Kinat had taught us the keys to dreams, I discovered we each had our own symbolic universe. For some things, my own keys were infallible. Had living in perpetual darkness, so close to death, given us a sixth sense, the right to gaze into the hereafter?

Some of my dreams were premonitions. Every time I ate couscous in a dream, a comrade was about to die. When I drank tea, something bad would happen to me. Fish heralded an argument, and Coca-Cola meant one of the convulsive fits I was prone to, caused by my gall bladder, which had me doubled up in agony.

As well as the ability to interpret dreams, Kinat had an obsessive habit: he would eat half his bread and stockpile the rest in a bag he'd made from scraps of fabric. He didn't realise that the other inhabitants of his cell, cockroaches in particular, coveted his treasure and took up residence in his bag. What bliss for those bugs, to live in a pantry! They laid their eggs and deposited their excrement there. Kinat ate this soiled bread and paid the price: his belly began to balloon, his pupils dilated, his teeth grew crooked; some curled inwards, others grew outwards or fell out altogether. He grew more and more monstrous and could only splutter, in a distorted voice. He could feel the changes taking place in him but could only see them in the guards' disgusted looks when they opened his door. Finally he died, poisoned to death, on 1 December 1974, borne off by his own instinct for self-preservation, but leaving us the keys to our dreams.

This death brought home the gravity of our situation: we were doomed to die of hunger, cold, vermin and disease, with no help and no compassion, no resources other than our faith, our youth, our capacity to endure and fill time.

The guards no longer attempted to cover up death; there were no more stretchers. Not waiting for the next mealtime, they came halfway through the morning, opened the door to the block and started digging in the yard. Then they entered the cell where our friend lay on the ground, half-naked and quite dead, rolled him up in his blanket, lifted it at each end and went out to throw him in the hole. They dusted him with quicklime, sprinkled water over him, put a sheet of corrugated iron on top and filled in the hole. They had done their duty like the good – blind and obedient – soldiers they were.

There was pain and suffering, moral suffering and that of the flesh. I knew the first and very soon encountered the second, when it attacked the thumb on my left hand. First came an itching sensation, then a little spot appeared between the nail's edge and the skin. Nothing too serious up to that point, were it not for the premonitory dreams in which I saw myself draining a large glass of Coca-Cola.

The spot became a boil and spread to the tip of my thumb and underneath the nail, which began to turn yellow. It was a whitlow; I knew they were very painful. It started with insistent stabbing pains, which became more and more intense. The pain wasn't continuous but rose and fell again in a regular rhythm.

Since fasting was no use in this case, I tried another remedy: yoga. To be honest, I knew nothing about the discipline except a few notions I'd picked up here and there by chance or in my reading. First I tried to control my breathing, then I concentrated on my nervous energy so I could direct it where I liked. I managed a control of sorts, enough that I could focus my attention on something other than the pain, and the result was successful… or almost.

The whole business lasted two months. Without much conviction, I pleaded with the guards to bring me a raw onion. Used as a plaster, it would have drawn out the pus and other impurities that were rotting my thumb. And, of course, it would have made a good antiseptic. My request was met with a sardonic refusal.

Finally, one morning, I saw that the rags I'd wound round my thumb were damp. I delicately unpeeled the makeshift bandage and discovered that the whitlow was hollow. It released a phenomenal amount of pus and a more fluid liquid that wasn't blood.

The pain had gone, but the struggle went on; now I had to watch out for infection. But how could I, with no hygiene whatsoever? I remembered being taught that saliva and urine were antiseptics. With my good hand, I cleaned the rags I was using as a dressing with a tiny bit of water – which itself was dubious – then I urinated on my thumb and the cloth strips, giving them a good soaking. It was free, after all. And I put it all back on.

This carried on for a month. Morning and night I washed my little strips of cloth – always the same ones, as I had no others and couldn't afford the luxury of taking any more from my own hide, since it was wintertime. I'd piss on it and dress the wound again.

I had bad bouts of fever, sometimes to the point of delirium. I sweated copiously. I felt – I knew – my body was fighting the infection; I needed to help it, to concentrate on each part of it, feel it living and palpitating, mobilising on behalf of the ailing extremity. I prayed, too; I wasn't afraid of death, I was at peace with myself and my Lord, but I prayed for the courage to bear it, to fight, not to complain, not to groan, not to distress my companions.

Great quantities of liquid and pus came out of the wound every day, as if all the accumulated vermin of this hellhole was escaping via my thumb. Little by little, my nail began to detach, until it came off altogether. Then the bleeding gradually stopped, the fever subsided and my thumb started to peel all the way to the base. It grew a completely new skin; it moulted and began to recover. The nail in turn began to grow again, young, clean and tender. Once it had entirely regenerated, it hardened and regained its original shape.

My body and I had defeated sickness and death, thanks to pee. To save every drop of saliva, I never spat and, as far as possible, avoided drinking the contaminated water we were given. I never let myself fart except under my blankets, so as not to lose the tiniest unit of heat. Now I was using my urine to disinfect myself. I had achieved total self-sufficiency.

A month and a half after the soothsayer's death, it was the turn of Baba Driss, a young NCO in the air force. He was an armourer and served under Al-Aïdi, who liked him a lot even before they were imprisoned. Baba's health was not good; he always looked pale, as if he couldn't shake a congenital jaundice or some disease of the blood. When he was arrested, he was unmarried. He spoke more, and more emotionally, about his hometown Taza than about his family. Out of modesty, no doubt.

His great friend in the block was Lieutenant Elkouri, a man who'd been in my year at the academy. They had very similar personalities. When they weren't listening to the morning news round, they held long discussions. Both of them were calm and considerate, and they got along extremely well. They would avoid controversial subjects and, when the atmosphere became strained, they'd close themselves off, taking advantage of quiet moments to have their own private conversations. At times, discussions in the block would turn sour over something trivial. Each man wanted to be right at all costs, even when the evidence was against him. It often came down to a disagreement between individuals, a bad day or the simple pleasure of contradicting someone. There are also those who, by disposition, always have to be right. They think they know everything, understand everything, and they enjoy lecturing others. In Tazmamart, if someone like that didn't quickly become aware of his flaw, which was as dangerous to his comrades as it was to him, he ended up becoming isolated or dying – which came to the same thing.

One day, for no apparent reason, Baba began to have absences, momentary memory lapses. He would lose the thread of a conversation and slip off somewhere else. Then he began hallucinating: he saw snakes, which existed only in his ill mind. Sometimes he was delirious. His memories grew progressively hazy. He would forget where he was, the people around him, the reason he was in this accursed place. He tried frantically to salvage his past, clinging to it as to a lifeline, but, viscous and sticky as the water we drank, it slipped through his fingers. The more he forgot, the more he hallucinated. He retreated into a fatal silence. Elkouri would call out to him in desperation, trying to make him speak. He was endlessly dredging up events they'd talked about together, rummaging through his friend's past for anything with enough force to bring him back, to capture his attention, reconnect the threads of his memories or simply stir an emotion… But it was no good. It was as if his memory had been dislocated.

His ailing mind could no longer provide him with the weapons he needed to defend himself in a hostile, inhuman environment – a forest whose every concrete tussock concealed enemies: hunger, thirst and cold, which came to collect their tribute of corpses.

Baba died slowly, ravaged by hunger and madness. Losing the thread of his life, he lost life itself on 26 January 1976.

After the deaths of Kinat and Baba, I had an inspired idea, which saved lives and gave rise to scenes worthy of *Les Misérables*. I appealed to warrant officer Frih, an ex-soldier who had served in the French colonial army like the rest of the guards. Frih was more cowardly than he was mean – which to my mind was worse – but he could be useful if you knew how to approach him. I asked him not to throw my friend into the quicklime ditch with both his blankets; they need only drag him, as they usually did, using one blanket, and allow me to take the second. To my great surprise, he agreed. His generosity even extended to going into the dead man's cell, picking up all the rags he found and handing them to me.

As soon as the guards had left, Achour, who kept an eye on everything I said and did, shouted aggressively, "Hey, BineBine! What did the warrant officer give you?"

I kept quiet. I knew he was sick with envy; by saying nothing, I was putting pressure on him. When he reached boiling point, I called out to Dghoughi and explained my ploy. He thought it was a good idea and we laughed about it. But that day I'd opened Pandora's box, because now, as soon a death was imminent, the rag wars broke out. Everyone wanted the dead man's scraps. The survival instinct was justifiable, but approaches differed. Some acted tactfully and modestly, others did not bother with conventions. The guards, who had all entered into it, eventually imposed order by favouring the dead man's immediate neighbours and those who may have helped him towards the end, which was fairer.

*

This circulation of rags made me realise something: how far our sense of smell had developed. I noticed that each rag that I came across kept a very distinctive smell, its owner's. So now I could recognise another man's smell. I began to occupy myself by classifying these odours and memorising them, those of the dead and those of the living, at least the living with whom I had any dealings. The lessening of one sense sharpens the rest.

One comrade, who was good with his hands, took advantage of a rare day when we were allowed to sweep our cells to rip a bit of metal from a sheet of corrugated iron that we used for picking up rubbish. He sharpened it, turning it into a razor to cut his hair and beard, which had grown too long and made him look like a caveman, which in fact is what we'd all become. He made more of them and, as soon as we had the chance, we all cut our hair as best we could. When my turn came, I picked up the pseudo razor blade and spent hours sharpening it on the only smooth surface in the cell, the concrete block. Trying it out, I understood why it hadn't aroused much enthusiasm: it ripped the hair out more than cut it. The stoics among us used it; the more sensitive types, like me, preferred to keep our pelts.

But the invention wasn't wasted: someone else had the idea of making a needle from the metal shard. We cut the strip of metal as narrowly as possible, tapering its point with the help of a bit of concrete we dislodged from the wall, then we rubbed the middle of the opposite end until we made a hole – and we had our needle. This took time – months of patience and work, with its share of failures and moments of doubt and despair – but, in the end, we succeeded. Not once did anyone abandon their 'rock'. We'd passed from the Stone Age to the Bronze. We could sew. We sewed our old rags together and made hats, slippers and waistcoats. We didn't eat our dead, but we weren't far off; we clothed ourselves in their tattered flesh.

These new husks protected us from cold in winter but not from reptiles and pests in summer, and there were many different kinds: snakes, tarantulas, scorpions, various lizards and cockroaches. On the other hand, there were no insects, flies or mosquitoes, no fleas, bugs or lice; these last were bloodsuckers and had apparently died out in our block. Either that or our block was so destitute it held no appeal, or might poison them.

We learned to live with these unpleasant creatures. Deprived of sight, our other senses had become more acute, especially smell and hearing, so we could identify the sounds and smells that filled our solitude. Very quickly, we were able to tell one creature from another by its sound – except for the large spiders, which didn't make any. But they never came into our cells, so they didn't worry us as much as the scorpions, which could kill. Among their victims was Thami Abounssi, a young lad from Safi, an air traffic controller. Thami was sweet and kind, the level-headed type who didn't draw attention to himself, spoke when he had to and kept quiet when the moment demanded it. One evening, around dusk, he heard the very recognisable sound of a scorpion falling. Aided by the rough reinforced concrete, the beast was climbing up the wall, reached the ceiling and there, not managing the bend, fell back to earth with a tiny thud very different to the one made by cockroaches, which could cling to the ceiling but, when they dropped, chose the shortest way down.

So Abounssi heard the scorpion fall and alerted us.

Whenever danger threatened, the entire block would mobilise to find a solution or give auditory psychological support, the only possible help at that moment. Sustained by his comrades' voices, Abounssi spent all night tracking the dropping sounds, by turns closer or further away. When the sound came too near, he wrapped himself in his blanket and kept stock still, suffocating in the dry heat of the pre-Saharan summer. He only breathed again when he heard a far-off little thud.

This went on until morning. No one slept that night; we were all attuned to Abounssi's every move. Eventually, after one of Tazmamart's longest nights, the guards arrived. We'd never been so glad to hear them coming. When they opened our comrade's cell, he asked them to leave the door wide open so he could locate the scorpion, and they reluctantly did so. After a while, sensing the fresh air coming through, the scorpion made for the door. Abounssi spotted it and, instead of letting the guards crush it under their big boots, he launched himself furiously at the beast, as if in revenge for what he'd been through all night, and tried to stamp on it with his full weight. But in his rush and the dim light, he only caught the front of the creature with what was left of his sandals, leaving the tail free. In a defensive move, the scorpion stung him, injecting a good dose of venom. It died, but Abounssi went through hell. We begged the guards to help him, to call for a nurse or at least tie a tourniquet around his leg. As usual, they were deaf to our pleas and for forty-eight hours Abounssi had to endure the torments of the poison. But he didn't die of it any more than Haifi had, who'd been stung before. At Tazmamart, death was in no hurry.

One day, a comrade shouted to a guard, "Be a man and kill

me!" The guard answered, "I'm not mad enough to do you the favour!"

Like some of the others, Abounssi had no obvious illness, he'd just had enough. At the end of his tether, he had nothing to cling onto any more; his heart wasn't in it. He no longer spoke. He had no appetite, no strength left to fight. He let himself die like a caged gazelle and passed away on 13 January 1977, a month before his friend Elkouri.

*

Mohammed Elkouri was in my year at the academy, and was my friend. We remained friends until the last day, although our personalities could hardly have been more different. He was taciturn and discreet with a sad look about him, as if weighed down by a heavy secret. At twenty, he already had white hair, which made him appear serious and mature. Yet Elkouri loved a wild night out, though not with just anyone. He chose his few companions, of whom I was one, with care. But I only knew him to have one real friend. In Tazmamart, he gravitated towards Boutou, Abounssi and Baba. Like the latter, he started hallucinating. He spoke earnestly, held coherent conversations and, from time to time, thought he saw a snake in his cell. Even though his friend Baba had had the same visions, we still believed Elkouri the first few times, because snakes, scorpions and tarantulas were so common in summer. And anyway, nothing surprised us any longer in Tazmamart. Everyone expressed their opinion, and Elkouri's best friends made a joke of it. But as the days went on, the problem worsened. The snake grew bigger and bigger. Next Elkouri was hiding under his blanket and telling us how heavy the reptile was as it slithered over his motionless body. At other times, he saw the enormous creature in the cell's ventilation holes or disappearing down his toilet. We realised he was losing his mind, but the strangest thing was that he was aware of it too. In his lucid moments, he asked for advice and everyone offered solutions. Most often this was to trust in God and the Holy Qur'an. We suggested he recite the Al-Fatiha and Al-Yassine suras as often as possible. His delirium escalated, he saw more and more snakes, then he started talking to himself. He had long, often muddled, conversations with his father. Finally he reached the most dangerous stage, that crucial moment when we tip into accepting death, when our will breaks and we refuse to fight or even just to go on living.

He stopped eating, stopped covering himself, right in the middle of winter's macabre harvest. I recognised the urgency of his condition and, since he had flashes of awareness, I thought he should try some autosuggestion. I asked his immediate neighbour, Moha Boutou, to have him repeat constantly, "I must cover myself", "I must eat", "I must fight". Moha trotted out these affirmations relentlessly, but it became more and more difficult to attract Elkouri's attention. Then Moha stood on top of his water pitcher, his fingers clinging to the holes in the wall, and shouted at the top of his voice, trying to drag his friend from the clutches of death, the clutches of cold, hunger and insanity. Moha yelled himself hoarse, though he barely had any strength himself. Elkouri died on the 6 February 1977.

Two months later, on 24 April, the harvest grew deadlier still, this time in our half of the block, with the passing of Rabh Bétioui. A staff sergeant armourer, Rabh was a veteran among the pilots, yet he was so young! A good man from the Oujda area, he was – like all natives of that part of the country – crude, frank and direct, but at the same time almost reticent. With his neighbour to the left, Elhadane, and Kasraoui, his neighbour opposite, Rabh had formed a group of wise young men, brilliant for their age and their level of education, well brought up and always helping others.

Rabh was the first to lose his grip. One fine morning, he started holding forth about spies, traitors and secret agents. We didn't know what he was talking about at first, but we soon realised he was going off the rails. He confided in his friends about some of their fellow pilots who hadn't been implicated in the coup attempt, saying he'd found out they were spies. So-and-so was an agent of the military secret services, planted there to report back and send them to prison; someone else was in the pay of the Algerians, with a mission to sabotage equipment. After fellow pilots, he started on members of his own family who were also working for the police or the Ministry of the Interior, or some occult force or another. He never named anyone in the block, apart from a few guards, who were Russian or American stooges.

Attempts to jolt him out of his paranoia came to nothing, and he slowly walled himself off in doubt and suspicion. He could not trust the guards, whose mission was to poison or neutralise him using substances derived from advanced technology.

He refused to eat – his fantasies were stronger than his survival instinct – and, accompanied by its faithful messenger the owl, death carried off our friend Rabh on 24 April 1977.

The prison governor wasn't an agent of the CIA or the KGB, nor was he the ghost that haunted our friend Rabh's anguished imagination. He was one Captain Elkadi, a former soldier who'd served as cannon fodder in the French army's shock troops, earning his rank as NCO for France and his officer's stripes as the regime's right-hand man; in other words, he carried out the dirty work. Newly promoted to captain as the needs of the cause – i.e. Tazmamart – dictated, he'd end his career as a colonel, the ultimate reward for services rendered unto Satan. The devil in this instance looked just like the notorious, terrible Colonel Fadoul, who'd acted as enforcer for the protectorate's gendarmerie and had sold them his soul. In our land, crime pays.

The first time one of our comrades fell ill, the guards went to report it to Elkadi. He reprimanded them, telling them not to notify him if a prisoner was ill, wounded or dying.

"Don't come to me," he said, "until he's dead."

The guards took him at his word and stopped bothering him, except on one occasion that upset them a great deal. These 'good Muslims' were deeply shocked by the obscene display of some of the inmates' scrawny backsides. It was true that the thin uniforms we'd received on our arrival at Tazmamart had been worn away by time and the daily rubbing of our skeletal buttocks against the concrete blocks, which we used as bed, chair and altar. Over time, our rags, which were scant protection against the cold, could no longer cover our guilt and shame at being exposed in this way, like animals. When the rations came round, some prisoners draped their dignity in flaps from blankets that had defied the years; others, like my neighbour Bendourou, saw the matter quite differently. They wanted to make the soldiers face up to their responsibilities, and they flaunted their wretchedness and gaunt, naked bodies to compel them to ask the commandant to come up with a decent solution to the problem.

The guards especially hated Bendourou because, three times a day, he'd confront them with the spectacle of his emaciated private parts. When they opened the door to his cell to hand him his meagre fare, his pot was always behind him; he would turn around slowly and bend over to pick it up, noting their exact position as he did so, then, just as slowly, turn around again to take his food, offering his equally abject front view. The guards swore, cursed and ranted at him, but they had no good reason to punish him. They could only call for Allah's protection against Satan and his accomplices.

Bendourou's gamble paid off. After a few years, several deaths and much recrimination, Elkadi decided to 'renew the kit'.

That day, the guards arrived looking very pleased with themselves, smiling broadly.

"We're giving you new clothes!"

Now they wanted to strip us of the coverings we'd accrued over long years, the rags on our backs and the bits of skin we'd torn from our dead brothers.

They did indeed bring us khaki canvas shirts and trousers (although the only new thing about them was that they were clean) and two blankets worn just as thin as the ones they'd given us on that first day. The drama began when everything had been distributed, since the guards' orders were to pick up our old clothes and burn them in the yard.

Opening the door of the first cell, which was Kouyine Amarouch's, they asked him point blank to give them his old clothes. Kouyine was thunderstruck. He didn't understand. He couldn't understand. They were asking him quite simply for his skin. These rags, like the layer of dirt covering our bodies, were part of us. To take them from us was to skin us alive. Kouyine refused to comply, so the guards rushed him and tried to rip them off him by force. He fought, flailed, screamed, telling them to take the new clothes and leave him his own. It was no good. They managed to take his old clothing from him, ripping the new ones in the process, and beat him up so badly that he never recovered.

The other inmates were pacing their cages, caught like animals in a snare. We were helpless, panicked, wounded; everything we'd built up in the way of courage, endurance and hope was collapsing on top of us. We thought we'd hit the bottom of the abyss and nothing worse could happen to us; we didn't yet know the extent of fate's malice and men's cruelty.

Like the others, I was frantic. My mind was going at full throttle; it was seizing up. What could I do? I was cornered, but I had some time – I was thirteenth. I tried to calm down and think; I couldn't. Should I fight them? They were stronger. Beg them, then? Yes, maybe beg. Who knows, they might take pity on me. Suddenly I had an idea: the toilet! Mine had no

U-bend. I quickly twisted my blankets into a coil and inserted them into the waste pipe, taking care to attach them to the water pitcher, which I put back over the hole. I stuffed some of the rags into the cracks in the wall, keeping back a flap of blanket and some bits of cloth to hand over.

Battle-weary, knowing there weren't enough of them to control these desperate lunatics, the guards gave up beating us and threatened to stop the meals of anyone who did not give them what they demanded. This did the trick.

When the senior warrant officer opened my door, he found a little pile right there. He swept the cell with his flashlight, saw nothing and, with an air of disgust, nudged the rags out with a broom. He knew I'd cheated, but he accepted the compromise.

The shrewdest of us got away with it; the others had no food for a day or two and eventually gave up part of their skin. The flaying was harsh but necessary.

Later, the guards would admit that these were their worst moments at Tazmamart. Whatever anyone says, it's never easy to finish someone off. I waited patiently until the next day to retrieve my treasure. I washed it as best I could and put it out to dry in the cell. It was dirty, it stank, but I'd saved my 'skin' in that gruesome winter of 1977, with its three deaths in a row.

A few years later, a similar drama took place, but this time the guards knew the score. They seized our rags before handing out the clothes. We were ready, too, and only gave them part of our covering. The drama was less brutal, but it was just as painful for us.

That was the deadliest of winters. It was slaughter. "To be or not to be" had no meaning any more; the boundary between the two was so blurred that death had become commonplace. We could smell it. Death has a smell, which we quickly learned to detect. Every time a comrade was about to leave us, he gave off a particular smell. As soon as it began to hover in the building, we knew his death was imminent. There were other smells, all of them pestilential, but that one was specific and easy to recognise.

It wasn't only smell that betrayed death's presence; it had other messengers. The first was the owl. About a month before someone died, it would come every evening at the same time, hoot for a while and then fly off until the next night. On the night of the death, it did not come, but waited instead for its next customer. There were also premonitory dreams. We were never sad when a comrade departed; we were relieved for him. We were convinced that the more he suffered during his death throes, the greater the injustice done him and the deeper the absolution for his sins. In short, we were dying as martyrs. To each his own beliefs, his own lifeline.

For us the year started in November, with the arrival of the bitter cold. 9 December 1977 began the dark saga of the year we will never forget: the owl had come to stay. The smell of death was permanent and the foreboding dreams kept coming. In my row, there was Allal Mouhage, a flight sergeant who, on that fateful day, happened to be on leave.

So what was he doing at the airbase? He was just hanging around! His fellow pilots had gone, and he was hanging around! His wife and little girls were waiting for him, they were planning to visit relatives, and he was just hanging around.

What was he waiting for? This was the question that nagged at him until he breathed his last. Yet the answer was simple: he was waiting to meet his fate. Because he loved his job, the atmosphere at the base, the noise of planes landing and taking off, the sound of the jet engines being tested by mechanics, the great hum of all this teeming life, day and night, as if in a bubble of its own.

Like all those who fly, he also felt somewhat apart, slightly outside of reality and the world. He saw himself in others' eyes as if looking in a mirror at his own image, which exuded poetry, mystery, adventure and heroics. He was heir to Saint-Exupéry, Mermoz and so many others.

He loved flying – it was his whole life – but that morning, while he was on leave, just passing the time of day, just hanging around, he was to fly for the last time.

"Flight sergeant, get yourself into gear and get stuck in!"

The order stung his face like a whip. It came from the base commander. How could he dispute an order? What would he say? That he was on leave? Then what was he doing there? Nothing; he was hanging around. He left his young wife, his little girls and a promising career, and ended up at Tazmamart because, that day, he'd been hanging around.

Like his fellow pilots, he was calm and good-humoured and didn't nurse too many regrets. Like all of us, he clung to his faith with all the energy of despair; day and night he prayed to God to protect his little family. He worried a great deal about his daughters' future and his wife now: she had no job, no experience or income, how was she managing to live? How was she bringing up the children? These questions gnawed at him from within, the way his stomach ulcer already gnawed at him.

The burning sensations began early on and worsened until they stopped him eating. Little by little, he wasted away until he died on 12 December 1977. He'd uttered no recriminations, no complaints – he hadn't made a sound – but he set the stage for the grimmest of Tazmamart winters. The list would be long. One period of mourning followed another with no tears, no cries, no resistance. We responded to death with prayer, to our losses by giving thanks; this was what the Qur'an taught us.

Elhadane, who was a *fqih*, had helped Abdellah Lafraoui memorise the sacred text and left to him the privilege of teaching it to us. This ascetic man was discreet to his last breath, barely speaking unless it was to correct us on passages from the Holy Book. Then one day, a miracle occurred: Elhadane asked to speak. We were stunned, we fell silent; in this deathly hush he called out to a comrade and unleashed a torrent of abuse, which astounded us as much as it did its target. For a moment, we were speechless, then the whole block erupted in laughter.

That morning, the man on the receiving end had argued with his neighbour opposite and, in his fury, had flung the radio – which one of us had procured with great difficulty

– into the corridor. We were distraught. This was a disaster. No more news from the outside world. And what about the guards, how would they react? Any of us who had a bit of wire that we'd pulled out of a broom, or a thread of wool from a blanket, passed it to him through the holes in the wall. The poor man in the cell opposite was beside himself. For a long, long morning he tapped untold reserves of ingenuity in order to retrieve the magic box and only succeeded a few minutes before the guards arrived. The relief was tremendous, just like the anguish we had suffered.

Elhadane was one of those who suffered least in Tazmamart. He behaved normally, moved about, ate his rations, all the while knowing that he was ill. Nearing death, he began craving a date. He dreamed of tasting a date; it was his last wish. The others, too, had had a last wish, something they desired more than anything in the world. I understand why people sentenced to death are granted a last meal. We begged the guards to bring him a date, just one date. It was no use. We explained that the Prophet commended giving alms, "be it only half a date". To no avail. In the first week of January 1978, Elhadane carried his frustration away with him.

If, having lost everything, we still hope for something, we set ourselves up for frustration and disappointment, like the child who waits for something his parents cannot afford. I'd often think of the story of the poor woman who, with nothing to give her family for supper, filled the cooking pot with stones and water and put it on the fire, persuading her little ones that she had potatoes cooking. The famished children curled up near the pot and fell asleep, waiting for the meal. Moha Boutou was like those children; he was waiting to be freed, but less patiently.

He was a friend from my year at the academy, a Berber and native to the region we found ourselves in, near Gourama. He knew the terrain here and described it to us in great detail when we arrived, along with the vagaries of the climate, which we'd soon discover to our cost. Moha had studied at Azrou College, a place that had made headlines during the protectorate at the time of the Berber Dahir. The French had attempted to separate Berbers from Arabs in order to divide – and so rule – the country; their official language would be Berber, and they would have *aourf* law, a set of traditional unwritten rules, probably pagan in origin. But the plan collapsed, rejected by both communities.

And so Azrou College had been established to accommodate the sons of prominent families, indoctrinating them to form a pro-French elite.

After independence, the college was reclaimed by the government and renamed Tarik Ibn Ziad School. It still admitted Berbers from the region, but no longer made a distinction between boys from wealthy families and those from poor families. Teaching was provided by Jesuit priests who lived nearby in Toumliline. Besides instruction, they offered room and board to the very poorest. In return, these boys were expected to attain high marks in class and work in the monastery alongside the monks. Moha was one of those privileged few, able to study thanks to the priests and in particular thanks to Father Gilbert, whose saw him as his protégé. He felt a quasi-religious gratitude towards him, something that never affected his faith in Islam – as we could all attest.

Years later, Father Gilbert and his brother monks were, rightly or wrongly, accused of spying. They were expelled from Morocco, leaving the monastery and many young minds to languish alone.

Thanks to his excellent results, Moha was awarded a scholarship and became a boarder at the school until his baccalaureate, which he passed successfully. He then entered the academy, graduating as an officer and thus perpetuating the tradition of Azrou College being the incubator for most of the Moroccan army's highest ranks.

Moha was a calm and thoughtful boy. Self-effacing and tactful, he only intervened opportunely and wisely. At Tazmamart, his character did not change. He only made his presence known towards the end of his sentence. He'd been given three years and, the nearer the time came, the more nervous he was. When the fateful day arrived, he demanded his release. In vain. He came up against a wall of silence and indifference, and even provoked contempt because, not content with still being alive, he had the impudence to demand his right to be free. One day a guard, taking a philosophical view of his predicament, made this observation, "If you find yourself at the mercy of your Moroccan brother and he kills you, he'll have done you a favour."

Moha asked to see the commandant. Silence. He made such a fuss about it that he irritated the guards who took a hard line, depriving him of a meal and threatening worse if he went on asking for the moon, like Camus' Caligula. It was a shock to him; he couldn't reconcile himself to being detained illegally. Moha had been sentenced by a tribunal, *their* tribunal, a kangaroo court with kangaroo laws. He had served his time.

It took him a long while to accept his situation, and none of us could help, since his prolonged imprisonment was a slap in the face for all of us. What was happening to him would happen to us. No one would leave this place alive. The reality was cruel. We had to take it in, digest it, let ourselves fully absorb it; it sliced like the blade of the guillotine.

Moha was very close to mental breakdown. He narrowly avoided it just as, one cell away, Baba succumbed.

Moha spoke up for the second time when Elkouri fell ill, as I described earlier. He struggled desperately to inspire him to go on living. Standing on his pitcher, he yelled in vain the magic words that should have saved his friend. Then he relapsed into silence. We were vaguely aware that he was ill but, since he didn't complain, no one paid any attention until 13 January 1978, when he left just as he'd lived: discreetly.

Death went on brazenly taunting us. The foreboding dreams multiplied, the owl persisted in coming back every night to remind us that the lethal harvest was just beginning and, although three of us were gone, the smell of death hung in the air. All this plunged us into turmoil and confusion. We had no idea who was about to go on the ultimate journey, who was next on the list. We didn't know that death, arrogant and disdainful as ever, was going for the double, just to show us who was boss: Kouyine and Lyakidi on the same day.

Kouyine Amarouch was a small weather-beaten man from the Rif. What made him stand out were his pale, almost blue eyes and the dark complexion that hid very white skin under a tan. Rightly or wrongly, his European look lent weight to the theory that some of the Rif Berbers are descended from Germans. Belonging to the Rif clan had been an advantage to Kouyine, allowing him to rise through the military hierarchy. And like everyone under Ababou's command, he'd come from the ranks of the French army.

Kouyine had criss-crossed all of Morocco, which he knew as well as he did Algeria, where he'd gone at the age of fourteen to work as a farm labourer. At that time, the colonisers employed a large seasonal Moroccan workforce, mostly from the north. He knew only Algerian popular songs or military tunes, dirges that evoked the melancholy of villagers snatched from their lands, their ploughs and their ancestral traditions to be hurled across oceans and worlds they never even knew existed and used for cannon fodder. I regret not having had the memory or attention necessary to learn those songs, which were subtly ironic and narrated a whole segment of our history. Unlike Ababou's gang, or the guards', Kouyine had not been a *goumier* – a Moroccan in the French army – but a *spahi*, one of those horsemen in a great white *burnous*, the aristocracy of the French colonial army. Their lives were no happier or easier than the others'; they too charged head-first into the open jaws of Uncle Ho's cannons, waded deep into the marshes of the Mekong Delta and lived their share of the horror. Kouyine had been taken prisoner by the Viet Cong but, according to him, he and his fellow soldiers were treated a good deal better than their French masters, as their captors called them: they got away with a little brainwashing or, more accurately, a course in political morality – if politics can be said to have any morality – which was supposed to open their eyes. They were taught that they, too, were a colonised people, and so France was their common enemy. However, their paymasters' brainwashing was obviously more effective since, apart from a few deserters, the vast majority remained loyal to France.

So Kouyine had already experienced prison. He'd seen his peers suffer and die. They were even forced to attend torture sessions and executions so they'd learn that all men really are equal when confronted with horror and death – the rest was just a question of dignity.

In Tazmamart, Kouyine proved very adaptable and easy-going, sociable and scrupulously respectful of our block's conventions, all qualities that our living conditions demanded.

He made us laugh when he related his adventures in Algeria, in Vietnam and even in Europe, since he'd been garrisoned in France and Germany. He also knew when to be quiet, which was vitally important for communal life.

Kouyine surrendered his soul on the same day as Lyakidi. He too fell into a kind of lethargy. He no longer responded to our calls, almost never ate. Had he lost hope? Was he hanging on to what he'd left behind? Or had some untreated illness consumed him from the inside? Little by little he wasted away until his death on 12 February 1978.

Perhaps he'd grown used to hunger; its quicksand was one of Tazmamart's great traps. When we went a few days without eating, we lost our appetites and, as time went on, we felt good – too good, filled with a pleasant numbness similar to a high from drugs. We no longer cared about food. This happened to me when I had trapped wind; for eight days my stomach was swollen like a balloon. I felt extreme pressure around my anus but, when I went to squat, my insides were silent, nothing moved. I was constipated by a gas pocket that was blocking my entire system. I couldn't swallow anything. I became used to this state, and to hunger. I took little sips of water and spent most of my time lying on my side.

On the afternoon of the eighth day, while I was lying down, overcome by a strange inertia, I began to hear the others talking as if at the bottom of a well. The birdsong was muffled. I wasn't dreaming, I wasn't thinking; I was vegetating. Suddenly, I felt a little pocket of gas shift in my intestines like a tiny bubble rising from the bottom of a glass of water. It paused for a moment at the rim of my anus then timidly broke out, as if piercing a liquid surface. I held my breath. Everything in me strained towards this little miracle of vapour. I didn't know if I should contract and push, like a woman about to give birth, or sit back, try to relax and let my body take care of the rest. I went for the second option and it was a good thing I did because, a moment later, another bubble came along which, just as delicately as the first, burst into the open. I prayed, and I waited. Could this be deliverance? I was caught between fear and hope, but very soon another arrived, then another, then yet another; the pace picked up and then there was an explosion of sounds and smells. When it was over, I felt lighter than a bird and thought this one of the best days of my life. Happiness is relative, after all. After this ordeal, my insides began to behave normally again. But the hardest thing was going back to food. I had to wage all-out war on myself, physically, morally and psychologically, to be able to eat again. But life is always reborn on the other side of despair.

I was daydreaming like this when they took Kouyine away to bury him – or rather, to throw him in the hole. The soldiers left when the grisly job was done, but a troubled atmosphere hung about the building. Prayers for the dead man weren't as fervent as usual. A comrade recited some verses from the Qur'an, which we listened to in a silence heavy with foreboding. Indeed, a moment after the first man was buried, the guards came back. Amid general bewilderment, they made straight for Lyakidi's cell. There could only be one explanation, as we knew only too well.

Lyakidi Mahjoub was more commonly called Moulay

Mahjoub. Moulay is the title given to descendants of the Prophet, the sharīfs. He wasn't a sharīf, though; the name was used somewhat pejoratively. Lyakidi was in my year at the academy and he didn't exactly pass unnoticed. He stuck his nose into everyone's business with an attitude that was pure Marrakech, which, in spite of everything, endeared him to us. He was Marrakchi to the tips of his fingers. Brought up in the medina, he'd inherited its vividness, its special sense of humour, its irony that verged on arrogance and its highly colourful language; he had a fake drawl and a talent for sharp repartee. He also knew a great number of sayings, quips and jokes, some good, some not so good. Most of the time, he was joking with his friends, even in the most dramatic situations. He'd often repeat a popular saying, "When you're surrounded by your friends, death is a picnic." Like most of those who'd drunk too much of the water we were given, he fell victim to dysentery. When he sensed he was near the end, he let us know. His friends in the neighbouring cells made sure to tease him about it, trotting out his favourite phrase. He died slowly, little by little, as if emptying himself, on 12 February 1978.

In the depths of that pitiless winter, that same February, who was the owl waiting for now? My great friend, al-Aïdi.

Al-Aïdi's father was a stonemason, a powerfully built, dark-skinned man. His size and strength were equalled only by his apathy. Never violent or angry, he was often indifferent to what was going on around him. He only had one son but behaved as if he had a dozen. When the boy's mother died, his father didn't show much emotion. He observed the funeral rites meticulously, buried her with all due piety and moved on. Once the mourning period was over, he remarried. The boy cried for his mother, but eventually accepted his loss. He didn't question his father, knowing he would get no answers.

Children, especially orphans, have angels watching over them. Al-Aïdi's angel was undoubtedly his uncle, his father's brother and polar opposite; he was a kind man, always smiling, attentive and caring. This man saw his nephew's isolation and distress and spontaneously decided to take the boy under his wing. After the father remarried, the uncle stepped up his visits, especially in the evenings, since tradition prevented his coming in the daytime while the man of the house was out. He said he was asking after his brother's health and morale, but the father wasn't fooled: he knew the visits were about his son. It suited him, knowing that someone was giving the child what he himself could not.

After a while, the stepmother showed a desire to mark out her territory, a desire that soon became all-consuming. She forced her stepson into a poky little back room and reduced his furniture to the bare minimum. Since his father didn't come home during the day, she seized her chance to drive the boy out of the house. When he objected that he needed to do homework or revise, she flung it back in his face, jeering, "Follow your father's profession if you don't want to fail, as they say," and burst out laughing.

Or even, "Did your father or your uncle go to school? No. So do what other kids do, go learn a trade and bring home some money. You're just a parasite. Go on, out! I'm sick of the sight of you."

And out he'd go. He went on going out, getting used to living on the streets, which became his true home. He knew every part of town, from the most hostile areas to the more welcoming. He made friends and enemies, learned to fight, to run away when he had to and to fend for himself; he became a man.

Living on the streets had an effect on him but so did his uncle, who did not judge, did not criticise, but merely pointed out the possible choices and different ways to avenge himself, not on people but on life. Victory over adversity would only come through education, and he would reply to his stepmother's sarcasm, "I'll learn a trade, yes, but from going to school."

So he knuckled down to his studies and worked hard until the day he was able to sit the entrance exam for the Air Force Academy. He became a trainee NCO, learned the job of armourer thoroughly and, after a training course in the USA, earned his stripes as a sergeant. Here was his revenge: he had triumphed over his background, risen through the ranks and become a warrant officer first-class, in charge of his section, competent and well respected. Al-Aïdi married very young and created the home he'd been deprived of as a child. He lived happily, surrounded by his wife and daughters, whom he loved above all else. He never neglected his filial duties; he visited his father and his stepmother regularly, found out how they were and what they needed. He also saw his uncle, whose kindness to him had never waned.

His father's death followed soon after his uncle's. On each occasion, he performed his duty conscientiously and buried each of them according to the rites and customs of Islam.

Once his father's funeral was over, his stepmother found herself in real need after a lifetime of marriage; she inherited only an eighth of the house and its contents. Since her late husband had received no state benefits, she had no pension and was left practically on the street.

When the mourning period was over, al-Aïdi visited her and proposed that she sell some of the furniture she no longer needed and move in to the upper floor of the house, which he would lease to her. She could rent out the ground floor and live off the rent.

He himself couldn't wish for more. He had his apartment, a wife who also worked, contributing to household expenses, and daughters they brought up with the utmost love. He was happy and bore no grudges against either his father or his stepmother. Or, moreover, against the destiny that dogged him, snatching him from his wife and daughters' love as it had robbed him of his mother's. Was he love's outcast, in perpetual exile from Eden? A heart doomed to wander in a wilderness devoid of affection?

In Tazmamart, he lived with dignity, struggled faithfully and courageously, played his part in the life of the prison and in establishing understanding, declaring that the better we got along, the better and longer we would live. He was always ready to tell a story or to sing – yes, we sang at Tazmamart; for us singing was a little corner of heaven in hell – tell an anecdote or talk about his family.

He'd survived the loss of his mother, his father's second marriage, the corruption of the streets and all the pitfalls of military life only to be defeated by a simple matter of hygiene and cleanliness when polluted water flooded the block – and yet God knows the filth we lived in.

One day, obstructed by who knows what, the drains overflowed into the cells and filled the corridor. The stench was unbearable, and prisoners were wading ankle-deep in excrement. Their lives were confined to the concrete blocks they slept on, and they used most of their water for washing their feet before they clambered onto their perches. Bizarrely, I was one of the few to be spared; in my cell, where the toilet had no U-bend, the drama should have been cataclysmic. In fact, each of the two rows of cells had its own drain, and they joined up outside in the septic tank, just below our block. The cells in my row that had been flooded were on the lower end, and the waters had seeped under the cell doors. This time, for once, the number thirteen brought me luck: an anomaly in the rough concrete floor caused a bump in front of my cell, thus doing me a great favour. I'd also taken the precaution of sacrificing part of my blanket, that most precious of possessions, to stuff in the gap under my door. Immune to our distress, the guards came in wearing their boots to give out our rations. Having no doubt been granted the authority from their superiors, it was a full three days until, early in the morning, they turned up with a pump to unblock the drain. They connected the machine using an external outlet and turned the pressure on. It was obviously powerful because a fountain of slimy, stinking sauce spurted from the toilet holes, spraying everything in the cells, including the little concrete islands on which my shipwrecked comrades had taken refuge. The guards were outside the building, jubilant at the power of their monster. When they came in to admire the results of their handiwork, they discovered the extent of the damage. The pump had only exacerbated the situation. They ended up unblocking the pipes using more conventional methods, and the next day they arrived with a garden hose and a broom to help the prisoners one by one clean their cells as best they could. After meals, this same broom was used to clean our plates.

The person who suffered most in this was al-Aïdi. It was the middle of winter, temperatures were below zero and no one was washing or performing their ablutions before prayers; we'd agreed that to do so was extremely dangerous. Al-Aïdi couldn't stand the putrid miasma any longer. He defied the danger and, without consulting with anyone, decided to take a shower. He washed himself with freezing water and, well, what was going to happen happened: he didn't manage to rid himself of the smell, since it had got inside him, but he caught bronchitis, which killed him.

Our friend wasn't the only one obsessed with the smell. The

guards were affected by it too, the warrant officer first-class in particular. On 20 February 1978, the day al-Aïdi died, he brought a bottle of ice pellets and sprinkled them copiously over his remains and the entire area, before dragging him in his blanket to his final resting place. It was the devil's alchemy, extreme unction in the form of ice pellets and quicklime.

"Be good, my suffering, quieten down. / You were crying for night; look, it's here now."* Yes, but our suffering knew neither night nor day. The worst of it was the cold: its bite was worse than a snake's and its sting worse than a scorpion's. Its venom penetrated the body's innermost cells; it was devious, cruel and destructive. It gnawed at us, sapped us, consumed us – it was taking its time, it knew its own power, it knew it would have the last word and would slowly destroy us.

In the most wretched moments of winter, I'd think of Siberian labour camps, of those who – under the tsars, or later, under Stalin – were deported there. I thought of the temperatures they faced and what they had endured, and my own suffering seemed less agonising. Human beings have endured and suffered worse.

Tazmamart indelibly marked us, its inmates, but no one connected with it came away unharmed. The guards, for example, were convinced the place was haunted. They were scared to come into Block 2 alone. The sentries claimed they heard cries and groans coming from our block, though we who lived there heard nothing. They also said they saw shadows wandering in the yard. One night, a large number of guards burst in while we were all sleeping peacefully, saying

* "Sois sage, ô ma Douleur, et tiens-toi plus tranquille. / Tu réclamais le Soir; il descend; le voici", from *Les Fleurs du mal* (1857) by Charles Baudelaire.

the lookouts had heard terrible screams coming from our wing.

Our own dead didn't haunt us, because we as a group had prayed for them in the darkness. We believed they'd passed into the other world.

Whereas, entrenched in their traditions and their blind convictions, the guards felt the lack of ritual and the absence of proper burial keenly, and so they *were* haunted. They fed their own terror. Tazmamart's purpose had been achieved: a myth had been born that would reverberate in the imagination.

Those guards were the dregs of colonisation, poor wretches who'd lost their souls after selling their consciences to a system that they'd never understood and of which they were mere by-products. This system had passed them on to another, which had sucked out what remained of their humanity. I feel sorry for them. I pity them. May their children never know what they took part in.

A few of them suffered misfortunes. Everyone suffers misfortunes, but when you have a guilty conscience and you're superstitious, you believe bad luck is a curse. This was especially true for warrant officer Ben Driss, who lost two children one after the other in accidents. He was one of the most ruthless guards, like Sergeant Salah, who arrived as a corporal. Salah was a nasty piece of work, of average height and skinny with a hint of femininity about him, which he resented. Even the men who worked with him were afraid of him – they suspected him of spying on them and reporting back to their superior. Sergeant Salah fell off a ladder and fractured his pelvis. He spent a year in hospital and never walked properly again.

Both of them came to us, in tears, to ask our forgiveness. They also requested transfers, both of which, unusually, were granted. But on the whole, the guards didn't leave Tazmamart either: they were condemned to stay with us to the end.

Although they lived in far better conditions, their fates were linked with ours and they hated us for it. They often acted in an un-Islamic way, but one of us, Elkhadir, was watching them. He had a privileged position: he was in the cell right in front of the main door at the entrance to the block and, through a peephole, he witnessed many incidents that he related to us in minute detail. He saw the first burials and informed us about their methods for burying the dead – the quicklime and the corrugated iron.

Every day, he witnessed the cooking pot being cleaned with the broom that was used to sweep the floor; on the day of the flood, he saw them do this after sweeping away the sewage. He also often saw the guards picking cockroaches out of the soup.

One day, the guards found a dead rat in the pot; they fished it out with a ladle, threw it away and served the lunch with no qualms whatsoever. Another time, they found a scorpion. That day, they were serving one of the better meals. Elkhadir told us about the scorpion after the guards left, but we decided unanimously and without hesitation to eat it anyway. Meat was rare and these improved meals were served only when the king was celebrating an important family occasion; then they would let us share the joy of the Moroccan people. It was camel meat and it smelled bad. The other prisoners said camel meat always smelled a bit, but I knew that wasn't true because I'd eaten it in the past. Even though I was hungry, I didn't touch it and my neighbours were more than happy to eat my share. I wouldn't be surprised if it was responsible for a few cases of dysentery.

Elkhadir, alias Aboumaakoul, was one of Ababou's lot. He was from the Rif and from the same tribe as his chief and brother-in-law. A warrant officer first-class, he was in charge of vehicles and equipment. He and the son-in-law of warrant officer Akka ran the more lucrative end of the business. Elkhadir despised his subordinates and loathed his superiors with a passion; apart from his master, no one was fit to tie his shoelaces, nor was anyone as worthy as he to wear officer's stripes. He was a Berber and detested Arabs. When I saw him, I always wondered if he didn't hate himself – to say nothing of the guards and whoever had had the guts to throw him in prison. Like Bendourou, he chose to withdraw into himself. He didn't take part in prison life, had neither friend nor confidant. He attracted our attention when, to a guard who reproached him for answering in French, he said, "If I can't speak my own language [Berber], I'll speak whatever language I like."

Was this a sign of spirit or of bitterness? Elkhadir died on 21 April 1979, succumbing to dysentery and all the rage he carried inside himself.

*

Ultimately, the Skhirat expedition was a family affair, a matter of clans and tribes, not to mention a settling of scores between the monarchy and the people of the Rif. And yet many of them had taken part in the bloody repression of the Berber insurrection in the north in 1959.

Colonel M'hamed Ababou had dragged his whole family in his wake: his two brothers, neither of whom were part of our unit – his older brother, Mohamed the colonel, and Abdelaziz the sergeant – as well as three of his brothers-in-law: Aboumaakoul the warrant officer and two other NCOs I didn't know except by hearsay.

Seeing them united in this insane venture, you would have thought that the Ababous – a very large family – were very close. Far from it.

A month prior to 10 July 1971, after much haggling, argument and compromise, the entire family had gathered in the presence of their father, who was still alive, to work out what their share of the inheritance would be when he died. A week before the events, they assembled again in the paternal home to finalise the agreements they had signed, happy that the business was at an end. They had no idea then of what fate had in store for them. Three brothers and brothers-in-law would die, some at Skhirat, the others in prison, and, in line with Muslim law, it was their father who finally inherited from them! Talk about counting your chickens… M'hamed's hide was worth a lot more than the others'. He left behind a real fortune, and rumour had it that, on the day his will was read, a wife emerged from nowhere to claim her share.

Colonel Mohamed, however, was not rich. If you knew him, you'd wonder how he could have been caught up in his brother's net. As for Abdelaziz, who was just an ordinary sergeant – a pen-pusher attached to some office or other at headquarters – all he did was pick up information that would benefit his illustrious elder brother. He had no idea of the consequences of his actions. Abdelaziz was in the cell next to mine and, until the day he died, he never knew whether to hate or admire his brother. In Tazmamart, he tried to be inconspicuous, as if to make people forget the terrible name he bore. He'd left behind a wife, children and a career, which – if not brilliant – would at least have guaranteed him a decent life and a share of the inheritance he'd only ever seen on the parchment paper of an *adoul.**

Abdelaziz was doomed by the blood in his veins, since he was the younger brother of our chief, the colonel, the one who started the whole thing. He was cut down in the deadly harvest of that winter of 1978, on 1 November, dying of hunger, cold, vermin and inertia.

* A public official certified by the government to draw up documents such as marriage certificates and civil contracts.

One day I had a visitor, a ray of sunshine in my solitude. It was a type of sparrow we called Tibibt, because of the sound it made: *tibiiiiiiib*. This little bird from the hotter regions is sacred to Moroccans. When we were young, we were taught to respect it. We called it 'Lalla' Tibibt and no one, not even children, dared attack it for fear of committing sacrilege. In English, it's called a bunting, I think.

I was glad of the visit, so without a second thought I decided to put a few crumbs from my frugal meal into the ventilation holes he'd entered by. This relationship lasted for years. Tibibt made my cell his home: he'd spend the night with me and come to eat throughout the day. The prison block was home to many birds, but we didn't see them. They lived in the area above the cells, under the corrugated-iron roof. We heard them cheeping all day long. In the beginning, it was a deafening, chaotic din. Little by little, we learned to identify the songs of different species. We didn't know their names or what they looked like, but we could tell them apart by the sounds they made, the same way we had with our friends the pilots in the early years, who were outside our field of vision. We knew everything about those men, about their lives and families; we could even tell which one breathed, without ever having seen their bodies or faces. Whether they were fat or thin, big or little, we'd never know. They existed only in our ears.

As for the birds, we learned to recognise – or rather to decipher – their songs, their language. There was one sparrow, always the same one, who, just before the guards arrived, would utter a series of strident screeches; the others kept quiet for a moment, then answered her in chorus. I don't know why I was convinced she was female. The guards would come two or three minutes later. This always happened, whether they came at the usual time or unexpectedly. We'd been warned. Our winged neighbours also announced the weather two or three days in advance. There were different songs for rain, storm or sandstorm; the sparrows were the ones that sensed things most acutely. And when a snake entered the block, whether through the door or the roof, they would sound the alarm.

I discovered that my Tibibt had two very distinct songs: the ordinary one that everyone knew and to which he owed his name, and another that took me a long time to recognise. The day my neighbours opposite were about to be transferred to Block 1, he came to my window (which was what I called my air holes) and kept repeating an unusual cry. He went on like this for several days until our comrades left. They made way for some African men who would stay with us for some time. Afterwards, Tibibt went back to his old song. From that day on, I recognised that call announcing someone was leaving, whether it was a guard, our African guests, our transfer to Block 1 before we were freed, or freedom itself.

In 1979, Cold and Death moved in, taking up their winter quarters to claim their due. The deadly tithe of bodies hadn't yet begun when, one afternoon, the duty sparrow heralded the guards' imminent arrival. For a few minutes, men and birds stopped chattering and there was a stunned silence. The darkness must have obscured the looks of amazement on inmates' faces as they asked themselves countless questions about why the guards were coming. Then the birds took up their cheeping chorus, a deafening din that ended, as it often did, in a collective beating of wings. Only the fledglings, which had stayed put, called timidly for their beakfuls of food.

Soon after, the guards came, opened up some cells and ordered their occupants to pick up their things: a few rags, a pitcher, a pot and a plastic plate, covered in all the grime of their years of misery. Moving to the other block! We were bewildered. What was going on? Why this sudden change? We didn't expect to be told anything by the guards, who didn't say a word, not out of loyalty to their superiors but fear of them: we were living proof of what could happen to them if they didn't strictly obey orders. A coward is more dangerous than a cruel man.

Our comrades left. How had they chosen who would go? We'll never know. I wonder if those who decided even knew themselves.

Things didn't stop there. After they'd filled the empty cells in Block 1, the administration – needing to free up fourteen more cells – decided to put two prisoners to a cell for the last three or four. Was this luck or disaster? Imagine two people who have never seen each other, who've known each other only by voice, finding themselves shut up in a two-by-three-metre cell with just one concrete block to sleep on. Who would take it? The one who slept on the floor would constantly have to pick up his bedding. When would either use the squat toilet in the corner, with only the darkness to cover his modesty? There was only one walking diagonal in the cell – it was impossible for both men to use it at once – so who would walk, and for how long?

We also needed to agree on an order of priority for conversations: first between the two 'cellmates' and then with those outside.

There were endless problems and questions. It was Sartre's *No Exit*: six square metres of hell. There was a reason behind all this upheaval but, distressed by the changes and unusual activity – our hibernation disrupted, our benumbed minds and senses jolted – we had not asked ourselves what it might be.

Not long after nightfall, still shaken, we heard trucks entering the prison yard. Our agitation was not over, especially as the sleeping birds didn't warn us.

Our block was opened. Escorted by gendarmes, the guards brought in new prisoners and locked them up, one by one, in the vacated cells. I thought of the poor devils about to experience what we had when we arrived, with the stench of rotting corpses into the bargain.

Once the prisoners had been moved in, the guards went off, taking care to lock the main door. A deathly silence followed. The new arrivals must have been in shock and we, too, were stunned.

We were no longer thinking about ourselves or our tricky situation of two to a cell; we were asking ourselves a thousand questions about our surprise guests. We didn't dare to speak yet, to find out what was going on and make contact the way it's done in these circumstances. We thought that, in this extreme cold, the guards would be coming back to give them at least a blanket to cover themselves or to sit on until morning. And – why not – a hot meal?

An hour passed, then another. Nothing. Throughout the night, the temperature kept dropping. I knew the climate here and was aware that the slightest mistake would be fatal. I was very concerned about the poor men and asked Skiba, their nearest neighbour, to call out to them. No response. They were probably suspicious. Each of us tried in turn, but to no avail.

Then one of them called out to his fellow countryman in a language we couldn't understand. So they were foreigners, Africans to judge by the accent. Calls rang out from all sides and a few snatches of conversation passed between them. One comrade suggested they were Mauritanian or Senegalese; he'd heard the language before, down south. I thought that in either case, they would likely speak French, so I called out to them, "Hey, comrades! Whoever you are, listen to me: don't go to sleep tonight. Whatever you do, don't lie down on the ground or on the concrete. Walk, keep walking, don't stop.

Talk to each other so you don't fall asleep, talking will warm you up. Those men won't come back, they have no pity, you must rely on yourselves!"

There was a long silence and then, from the other end of the block, one of them shouted, "Comrades! Where are we?"

Grumbling broke out immediately and one of them, who seemed to be in charge, reprimanded him sharply in their language. Then they went quiet. I knew the man had just been called to order and wouldn't say another word. I told him we were in Tazmamart and gave him a quick rundown of the place and of what awaited them. Silence reasserted itself and each of us drifted off into his own sorrows and concerns.

The guards came in the next day as if nothing had happened, served breakfast with the daily bread and pitcher of water then went off, ignoring the poor creatures who were lying on the other side of those doors, frozen to the marrow, starving and broken by fatigue.

Halfway through the morning, they came back with everything the model 'Tazmamartian' might need: two threadbare military blankets; a pitcher, which they filled up; a plastic pot and plate. They shut the door again and disappeared. At midday, they returned, serving everyone the eternal broth, in which swam a few lone chickpeas.

It was December. We'd almost forgotten the owl, which had been coming to visit us every evening for a while now. Soon we'd wake up and have to face our situation and that of our new neighbours. When I recall that time, I can't help thinking of Kacem, one of our fellow sufferers, and of these lines by Lamartine: "Its faraway echo resounds in my tender heart, / Like a familiar step, or the voice of a friend."*

Kacem was the youngest and perhaps the wisest of us all. His voice resounded because of a spirit of solidarity and a self-denial that were astounding for his age. He was new to the army; he'd finished his armourer's training and had only been serving for a few weeks. A rookie, in other words, with a very strong personality. He became indispensable when we began the lessons from the Qur'an – which he knew as well as Abdellah or Elhadane – and his help was crucial when it came to putting the verses together in the right order. Later, he acted as intermediary, relaying the suras to our side of the building since we couldn't hear Abdellah clearly at our end of the corridor. Also, when we couldn't disturb the others, Kacem was careful to correct us and remind us of the exact wording.

As well as the Qur'an, he knew a lot of hadiths, the words of the Prophet written down by his followers. He had everything our parched souls needed in order to clutch at the hope of a hereafter that would be better than our daily reality. He was a lynchpin in the life of the group. Still, he suffered like everyone else, on top of which his tonsils were inflamed and made his life a misery, causing him many problems over the years. They were sometimes better and sometimes worse and gave him a permanent fever and periods of terrible feebleness that meant he couldn't climb up on his pitcher to deliver the Holy Scriptures.

* "Il résonne de loin dans mon âme attendrie, / Comme le pas connu ou la voix d'un ami", from 'Milly ou la terre natale' (1830) by Lamartine.

When his tonsils were too swollen, he couldn't eat or even drink, he couldn't swallow: he had chronic tonsillitis. One day, weary of the fight and without telling anyone, he decided to try to remove them.

From time to time, the guards would give us strips of corrugated iron to put our rubbish on when we swept our cells. We'd take advantage of this to wrench bits off them, which we'd sharpen and use for different purposes. Kacem decided to use one of these blades for his surgical operation. A narrow, fairly long sliver, sharpened for days on end. When he considered it ready, he put his finger in his mouth, located the offending appendages and at night, while everyone was sleeping, did the deed. We heard stifled groans, moaning and gurgling sounds. No one paid much attention; nights in Tazmamart were filled with every kind of noise, nightmare and anguish and, anyway, no one dared violate the rest time.

In the morning, Kacem didn't get up for his ration of bread and water. At that time, the guards wouldn't let anyone go to help an inmate who was ill. After they left, we called him, but there was no reply. We were worried, especially as we could hear him breathing noisily. What had happened during the night? It was only three days later that we learned the truth. His condition was deteriorating, he couldn't eat or drink, he was delirious with fever. Finally, he fell into a coma.

A few days before his operation, the owl had come, faithfully keeping its appointment. We were surprised since no one was seriously ill. Could the owl have got it wrong? Were its earlier visits down to chance? No. It had not been mistaken. Its predictions were indeed the harbingers of death, which would stop Kacem's voice resounding in our battered hearts.

The next morning at breakfast, the guards realised he was dead. The birds alerted us to their arrival mid-morning and, miracle of miracles, they'd brought water to wash the corpse and a shroud.

Moses had struck water from the rock and the Ayatollah Khomeini had struck fear into our tormentors' hearts. It was the year of the Islamic revolution in Iran, and Kacem was accorded a dignified burial; the shamefaced guards even muttered a few prayers on 19 December 1979, when they took him away. Islamic revolution or no, he did not escape the quicklime and corrugated iron.

We said prayers in his memory and recited verses from the Qur'an aloud. The stranger who'd addressed us the first time asked us what was going on. We explained the situation and, despite his friends' reproaches, he pursued the conversation. He told us he was a Muslim, as were three of his friends, and all the others were Christians. His name was Zakaria. All the same, he refused to reveal their identities or the reason they were here. We knew only that they were black and not Moroccan. From then on, only the Muslims spoke to us; the others immured themselves in their suspicions.

Although they didn't talk, they were smart enough to listen to our advice. Especially that first night: they all walked, except one of them, who was ill. He lay down on the cold concrete. Zakaria told us he'd been ill before he came, and that those in charge of the transfer were aware of his condition. They didn't lift a finger, had not even provided a blanket for the night. The next day he started coughing; a hoarse cough, which worsened as the days passed, becoming cavernous, like the death rattle of a wounded animal. Perhaps his friends didn't suspect anything, but for us the message was clear. Kacem had died and the owl kept coming every evening. The sick man no longer ate, could not get to his feet. Eventually he died, killed by Tazmamart.

One morning, because he no longer answered when they called him, the guards opened his cell. A guard went in for a few seconds, came out and closed the door. For those of us who were used to it, there could be no doubt. After breakfast, we discussed whether we should say some prayers for the peace of his soul. Some thought that since the dead man was a Christian, we shouldn't, others – and my voice was the loudest – declared that God is One and a soul needs prayer, whatever its language or religion. We won the argument and together chanted some verses from the Qur'an. A few moments later, the guards came in, took out the body which was rolled up in its blanket, and threw it into a hole with our dead.

Months passed; our guests didn't change their attitude towards us, but they were grateful for the prayer we'd said when their countryman died. They suggested we join them for a Te Deum, which we gladly did. The relationship ended there until the day they left, as abruptly as they'd arrived, leaving behind a corpse, the levy exacted by Tazmamart. That African, that foreigner who lies among our dead, is now part of our memory.

Of the nine comrades who had gone to Block I, one – Abdeslam Rabhi – would die there. Benefiting from fate's indulgence towards that block, Chaoui, Rijali and Dghoughi would survive. The other five would be returning to hell and, apart from Achour, would die here.

Their return followed hard on the arrival of another damned soul in Tazmamart. His stay there was as short as the story of his life.

That day, the block was calm; some were drifting in reverie, others lost to their nightmares, when the birds sounded the alarm. Their lookout gave a clarion call, announcing the imminent arrival of the guards at an unexpected hour.

For us, this was a godsend; any event or surprise – even an unpleasant one – anything that broke up the monotony of the prison was welcome. The padlock keys clinked, the bolts slid open and the guards burst into our block, followed by gendarmes dragging a poor wretch with his hands cuffed behind his back and a blindfold over his eyes.

Later on we would learn that the man's name was Miloudi Seddiq, a sergeant first-class in the Royal Guard – or perhaps the paratroopers, we weren't entirely sure; on the other hand, we were certain that he was one of the palace guards. Fierce, distrustful and disillusioned, Seddiq would not speak to us. He withdrew into himself, into a suspicious silence. He didn't talk to himself, didn't address the guards, didn't answer when they called him. Nor did he sing.

We only heard him for half an hour a day, breathing heavily while he did his exercises. We also heard a strange muffled thud, like a sack being dropped on the ground or thrown against the wall with some force.

What crime, what sacrilege had he committed to find himself in this hell? The mystery surrounding him deepened; perhaps the only people who knew for sure were those who sent him here – as well as Seddiq himself, of course, but he obstinately refused all contact with us.

Before he arrived, rumours had already been circulating that he would be transferred to Tazmamart; they added to the enigma of his imprisonment and struck mortal terror into the imagination. Wasn't terror the whole purpose of this deadly drama?

The Bourriquat brothers, who joined us not long after Seddiq, had told us this. Theories abounded. The first concerned an argument he'd supposedly had with a princess while on duty at the palace gate; some said he'd even insulted her. A second hypothesis was that he'd uttered death threats against the king, invoking a blood debt against the Rif people. But all this was speculation; only Seddiq and his antagonists knew the truth.

Life went on in Block 2 and Seddiq played no part in it. We only noticed him during his workouts. Then, one day, radio silence. No more noise, no more exercise, no more Seddiq. We worried about him, but our attempts to contact him still met with failure. We pleaded with the guards to find out how he was, but it was no good; as long as he kept eating, they wouldn't lift a finger. Although by that time, they had become more accommodating.

One day, when only one guard was on duty, I begged him to let me visit our recalcitrant neighbour to make sure he was all right. Fortunately, he agreed, and so I entered Seddiq's cell. You had to be accustomed to that gloom to make out the inert mass slumped on the concrete block. In a voice that was meant to sound firm, to show I wouldn't be giving up easily, I said, "*Salamu alaikum.*"

He muttered something and, to my great surprise, offered no resistance. On the contrary, I saw a kind of relief in the pale, distraught eyes staring at me – like a prayer. A look you might encounter on a winter's night in the eyes of an abandoned child. I picked up his bowl, held it out to the guard, who filled it, and approached him with the slop that passed for a meal. Still he didn't move. I was sure something was wrong and asked him, "How are you?"

For a moment, he didn't answer, then he murmured feverishly, "I'm all right, but you didn't have your meal."

It was true; in the heat of the moment, I'd forgotten my own. The guard had been so kind as to lock me in with my patient. Wanting to gain his confidence and make him feel more at ease, I answered, trying to sound casual, "We can share yours."

He smiled, tilted his head and uttered a little moan.

"What's wrong?" I asked.

"Nothing."

I saw he was trying to fob me off. I went closer and placed my hand firmly on his forehead. He was burning up. I gave him a severe look and said authoritatively, "Now, tell me what's wrong!"

He was evidently not intimidated. He looked at me kindly and said, "Eat."

"All right, let's eat together then."

I held out the bowl. He made no move to take it and suggested I eat first.

"I'll eat in a bit," he said. "I'm not hungry now."

All the time I'd been in his cell, he'd done everything in his power to hide something by his side on the concrete. He was trying so hard that he aroused my curiosity. I suggested helping him stand up, but he fiercely refused. So I pounced on his blanket and lifted it up. He didn't put up a fight; he no longer had the strength.

I found a large bundle wrapped in rags torn from the remains of the clothes he'd had on when he'd arrived. I put my hand on it and he let out a terrible howl. I jumped back, staring at him in bewilderment. He must have read all the anguish in my eyes at that moment. And I could tell he pitied me more than he pitied himself.

"It's my hand," he said. "I broke it when I was exercising and it hurts a lot."

"Can I see?" I asked in a voice no less stricken than his.

"Yes, but be gentle; it's very painful."

I approached him with enormous care and located his arm, my every touch making him cry out.

The more layers I peeled off, the more I gagged at the unbearable stench of rotting flesh. God knows we were used to the vilest odours of death and decay, but this was worse than any of them. I had a strong urge to vomit, but I was leaning over poor Seddiq. Under no circumstances could I show how I felt. Suddenly, there it was, enormous, bluish and suppurating, this wretched arm swollen with gangrene. It had tripled in size.

I thought I'd become jaded, hardened by Tazmamart. I'd seen death, felt death and come close to it myself, but here I was defeated, destroyed. Confronted by this sight, I felt so small, so powerless, so utterly bereft that my own suffering seemed laughable. I recalled a line from Tagore and turned my distress over to 'He who can bear everything', saying this prayer: "Lord, put an end to his suffering and grant him deliverance."

Yes, I wished he would die and, if I could have, I'd have picked up my saxophone or my trumpet and followed his funeral procession, like the musicians of New Orleans.

Taking turns, we sat with him and accompanied him towards his fate. During his exercise sessions, he'd let himself fall against the wall and catch himself with his hands; that was the dull thud we had heard. One day, he'd landed awkwardly and that's how it happened. Perhaps if he'd been treated in time, perhaps, given sedatives, perhaps… perhaps… perhaps… perhaps if he hadn't done anything… perhaps…!

It was just after the death of this solitary man, in the spring of 1980, that our comrades who'd been exiled to the other wing returned, at least those whom fate had cursed.

A few months after Seddiq's death and the return of our comrades who'd been moved to Block 1 when the Africans arrived, I fell ill. At first, it was a minor discomfort that came on at nightfall; my fingers would go slightly stiff for a few minutes and then loosen again. As this happened only once a week or less often, I wasn't too worried and I thought it would pass, like so many other ailments. How wrong I was. As the weeks and then months went on, the discomfort intensified, becoming stronger and stronger and more and more frequent. I waited for it. It signalled its arrival the night before in a dream, always the same, in which I was drinking Coca-Cola. The portents were never wrong. The second sign of impending crisis was that my penis began to shrink until it almost disappeared; when I put out my hand and couldn't find it, I readied myself for the onslaught. It began by taking over two of my fingers, the index and middle, then jumped to the thumb and finally spread to the ring and little fingers. After occupying my right hand, it attacked the left: my fingers tensed and became as stiff as wooden sticks, protruding in different directions. I couldn't control them. When I touched my face, it felt as if my fingers were dry twigs. Then my whole hand went numb, completely inert. No sensation, no reaction; it was no longer a part of me. I think it must be the same for trees' dead branches. The numbness gradually rose up my arms and, as it did so, the pain set in; a stealthy, radiating pain, first in the afflicted area, then throbbing in time with my heartbeat. It grew more insistent and eventually became continuous.

The attacks redoubled in strength. Now they came every night and paralysed my entire body; only my head was spared. I'd been reduced to a ball of pain.

When I realised how serious it was, I decided to organise myself. I had experience, now, of living in this tomb. I knew my worst enemy was not the illness itself; that didn't scare me – and nor did death, for we'd become so familiar. In situations like this, it was easier to die than to live. And more cowardly. It was crucial not to give in to the easy option, to stop struggling. I decided to fight.

As soon as the attack was imminent, the first precaution was to settle myself under my blankets in a comfortable, secure position to make sure that when I couldn't move, I wouldn't be leaving myself exposed and thus vulnerable to the cold for a whole night, which would have been fatal.

Once I was in a good position, I waited apprehensively for the attack to progress. It came on inexorably, invading my poor carcass, which was stretched out on its side – a creature in the fangs of its predator, awaiting the merciful moment that would deliver it from anguish and pain.

The paralysis spread along unvarying lines; I now followed it as one follows a well-trodden forest path. It settled in like an irascible mistress certain of dominion over her helpless lover. The pain came too. It was brutal and implacable, intensifying until it became unbearable. My body was nothing but this ferocious pain, from who knows where, yet my head was untouched. From the base of my neck to the top of my skull was a no man's land – no pain or paralysis, just my four other ultra-heightened senses, an appalling consciousness, pitiless clarity. My mind was alive, sensitive to everything that breathed, vibrated, moved and lived in my cell, in the block and even beyond. I could hear my comrades' breathing as they slept, the ones sleeping peacefully and those who tossed and turned; I could almost feel their dreams and their nightmares. I could hear the wind whistling as it rasped against the forbidding walls of this place of death and the moans and groans of animals exhausted by the winter cold. Then, at the height of my torment, as the attack neared its peak, I felt an immense breath rising up to the heavens, as if all nature were sighing. I called it the breath of night. At that moment, I'd reached the pinnacle – the paroxysm of pain – and hope was finally reborn… I'd gained the summit, dragging my cross; it couldn't get any worse, I was on the way back down. The nearer the sunrise, the looser the pain's grip became, but the process was desperately slow. At last I heard the faraway call of the muezzin for morning prayers like a call to freedom. Little by little, my body relaxed. I struggled frantically to drag my hand to my mouth, millimetre by millimetre. This was the price of liberation. It took two to three hours to claw my way across the three to four centimetres between my hand and my mouth. When positioning myself before the attack, I'd taken care to place my hand as near to my mouth as possible. Then I had to choose the finger most likely to manage the next operation and arrange my body as best I could to see it – given that I couldn't feel it – and, without sacrificing my position, I performed gymnastic contortions to attain a good sight angle.

Once I'd glimpsed the lifesaving finger, I contrived to incline my head so that it was easier to insert it into my mouth. Then I pushed my neck with all my strength to make my tongue slide along this bit of hard, cold, rough wood until it made me retch. As soon as I achieved this, I knew the battle was over and the end of my suffering was in sight. I maintained my position and kept pushing; the spasms came one after another, movements became easier, then I could insert my finger deeper into my throat until I was released: a powerful tide of bile rose from my gut, spurting like volcanic lava from the entrails of the earth, filling my mouth with a warm, horribly bitter liquid. When we threaten someone with the worst punishment, we say we will 'make them drink bile'. I have certainly tested the accuracy of the phrase, having swallowed that bile for months on end, day after day.

When I'd completely voided my stomach of those destructive juices, the pain and paralysis stopped, leaving no trace except immense fatigue and utter emptiness. My mind – which, throughout these long hours, had freed itself from the body's shackles – poured itself into the immensity of awareness like a river returning to the riverbed, at last resuming its place in the normal course of things.

I tried very hard not to cry out with the pain. What was the use? It wouldn't help; who, apart from my fellow inmates, would hear me? They were suffering just as much as I was and their sleep would only be broken, not by my shouts but by their own feelings of helplessness.

This happened at a time when the guards had become a little bolder and more humane and allowed us to help one another.

When my friend Daoudi came to see me in the morning, he found me weak and exhausted, incapable of standing. I was drenched from head to foot, and my blankets were soaking too. Daoudi gave me my water and food and helped me drink some coffee. He said he'd heard me groaning all night.

Staff Sergeant Baghazi was without doubt the nastiest of the guards, but he was also the least cowardly. He was on duty that day. At this time, one of our fellow inmates, Lieutenant Touil, was granted rare permission to walk in the yard. He managed to persuade Baghazi to give some money to Achour, who was from the same tribe as him. The wily Baghazi agreed. From time to time, when he was the only one on duty, he would buy Achour medication. Everyone in the building knew about this, but no one expected a thing from that particular individual.

One morning, when one of my attacks had lasted longer than usual, Baghazi witnessed my suffering. The sight clearly touched him because, when he was serving our meal that evening, he handed me a strip of some type of pill. He was bringing pills at random… How could he have known what we needed? Still, anything that came from a pharmacy would be good for our ravaged bodies. Who cared? Baghazi had given me a present and, what's more, had sneaked it from Achour's packet. Since he knew Achour kept an eye on everything he said and did, he called out loudly, "Take these pills, BineBine, and pray to God they cure you!"

In reality, he was issuing a warning to his customer: "If you have a problem with this, you'll have to answer to me." Achour took care not to protest immediately, but he could be heard ranting and cursing all evening. When he calmed down, he called to me, "Hey, BineBine! Did you get the pills I sent you?"

Normally, I'd have answered, "Yes, thanks," but just then I was in no mood to let him off. I'd been at death's door for weeks while he'd been receiving medication without once offering me any – though it wouldn't have saved me anyway. And now he was after a bit of fake gratitude.

I took those pills. During this stay of execution, they couldn't do me more harm. I was half-dead; the attacks were getting longer, more frequent and more violent; there was no way out.

One night, the attack was more vicious than ever. It began very early and intensified until it reached a frenzy. My body and my mind were entirely independent of each other. I was terrifyingly lucid. Utterly detached from my body, I was a spectator at my own death, because this really was the end. My heart began to pound harder and harder, racing out of control, palpitating so hard it made me forget the pain. Suddenly, a mysterious force tugged it with such strength I nearly passed out; then, with equal force, it let go. It went back to normal, like elastic. If I'd been standing, I would surely have keeled over backwards from the shock. A moment later, it started again. The force tugged, tugged, tugged… and my heart resisted. Yet I was ready to go. Every night, before getting into position, I'd perform my ablutions and say my prayers. I was at peace with the Lord and with myself. I thought of nothing, but simply observed what was happening which, in fact, no longer concerned me.

That night my heart refused to give up, in spite of the relentless assault of that thing trying in every which way to wrench it from its carcass. Battle-weary, death retreated. I pictured it, mournful and frustrated. It wasn't written that I should depart that night. No premonitory sign had foretold it, the owl had not come, and my first Tazmamart dream had just come true: yes, I was still buried, but I was also still alive. After that night, the attacks became less virulent and less frequent until they stopped. When I left the prison, doctors discovered what they called a 'necrotic' gall bladder; it had dried out around a cluster of gallstones. And in drying out, it had saved my life.

There's a character who weaves through all of Dostoevsky's work, *The Idiot* in particular. Lebedev has always fascinated me, since to me he represents the darkest part of the Russian soul. In Tazmamart, I had my own Lebedev, in other words the incarnation of the blackest, most devious and most complex part of the conscience of the Moroccan people and so, in microcosm, of our prison.

A Moroccan soldier from the ranks of the French army, Staff Sergeant Achour found himself randomly assigned to serve under Ababou, who considered Achour the ideal candidate for his purposes and accordingly had him join his infamous gang. To make up for his lack of education, Achour adopted a simple expedient that was as old as time: snitching. His motto was "*Anchouf angoul, ma nchouf ngoul qua même*": "If I see, I snitch. If I don't see, I snitch anyway". So he was a rat, a grass, a born spy, precious qualities that soon made him into the colonel's eyes and ears – but also, and much to Achour's fury, the eyes and ears of Akka, whose favoured position with the *maalem*, as they called the master, he deeply envied. Akka was his nemesis. Achour knew that, next to his rival's, his word was worth nothing. And so he decided to practise the principle of a saying he often quoted: "I kiss the hand I can't cut off".

Achour had the cell next to Driss Dghoughi, whose cell faced mine. I didn't know Driss or Achour – my two opposite neighbours – but, to judge by their behaviour, and not forgetting Bendourou's, I didn't stand much chance. Thanks be to

God, Driss proved to be a good man, who was fully conscious of the impact of his attitude on others and on their survival. He accepted his responsibilities and worked on himself seriously, which saved him in the end and – who knows? – perhaps contributed to the miracle of his recovery.

The best way to go beyond ourselves is by helping others; by solving others' problems, we forget our own. We learn to keep things in perspective and to go straight to the heart of the matter.

Achour took the opposite view. He thought only of himself, lived only for himself. He monitored everything. Woe betide anyone who spoke to a guard – he wanted to know what was said and whether the guard had ventured to give him anything. Oh no, Achour would not permit that; if a guard decided to do someone a favour, it had to be him or he'd rat on them. And he didn't mind letting the guards know this, which of course put them off helping anyone.

This behaviour annoyed and hurt many of our fellow inmates. They couldn't understand how a man would rather see everyone perish, himself included, than let someone else be helped. How could he not see that if the guards agreed to help one man, they'd end up helping all the others? Achour was consumed with envy. And envy, besides being a sin, is a real sickness, the cause of enormous suffering and extreme isolation. Add to that a good dose of illiteracy and years spent on the lowest rung of the social ladder accumulating inferiority complexes, and you have this mixture of nitroglycerine and bile.

He made others suffer, but his own suffering was even

worse. He didn't have the words to articulate it or any way to understand it. He could only express it in suicidal hostility.

I was the only support he had because no one would talk to him – still less help him – and yet I was perhaps the one he detested the most. Countless times I caught him inciting the guards against me, making up all manner of stories. But, thanks be to God, our souls were stripped bare and the guards could read them like a book. They knew us all too well to let themselves be fooled by a man like Achour.

In spite of his faults, he was shrewd and knew exactly where his interests lay. He was well aware I was his only lifeline, that without Dghoughi and me, he would be fatally isolated. So he pretended to agree to compromises. He would stab me in the back and endlessly praise me to my face. He knew I wasn't taken in by this and that I was well aware of what he was up to, but he also knew I wouldn't abandon him. He drank my stories to the last drop and never failed to interrupt me at the end to clarify something he'd missed or misunderstood. In the Qur'an study group, he found it impossible to memorise a third of the daily sura. In exchange for his keeping quiet during the session, I agreed to go over it with him afterwards. But his memory couldn't retain even an eighth of a verse, at the very most an 'Aya' or two, depending on the length. He tried to memorise a word by dissecting it syllable by syllable and, when he couldn't, he lost his temper, ranted and swore at me, telling me where to go – only to call out to me again a few seconds later and, without apologising, start up again. I accepted his bullying, his mood swings and his tantrums because I could imagine what a man with no culture or education, with no imagination and a shaky faith might be suffering deep in his dark cell, alone with his demons.

When the study session finished, he didn't thank me directly; he uttered a few kind words, or ones that were meant to be. He was good at flattery and kowtowing, but he was incapable of saying 'thank you'. If he did say it, he didn't know what it meant. He didn't know what gratitude was.

When the Africans arrived, he was transferred to Block 1, where he had an easier time of it. He benefited from medicines that were smuggled in, blackmailed people hand over fist and returned to us a few months later, perked up, along with Bendourou and Haifi. The atmosphere had changed: our ranks had been decimated, our health, memory, will and patience severely eroded. Achour shamelessly vaunted the delights of the other block, enumerating the privileges enjoyed by Lieutenant Touil thanks to the determination of his American wife, who had moved heaven and earth in the United States to procure her husband a special diet so he might stay alive. Touil and Achour were from the same part of the world and the same tribe, which Achour believed made them first cousins and entitled him to everything the other received. I found out later that Touil tried to be fair to his comrades and shared out equally part of what he was sent, which in any case was controlled by the guards.

When Touil was allowed out into the yard, he took advantage of the interval between the sentries' patrols to come and greet us at the door to the block. With the complicity of a guard, he even managed to slip us some pills of… who cared what they were? It was magical medicine that cured everything. We were so convinced of this, it became true. I was the proof.

These visits of Touil's poisoned the atmosphere for us. Considering the lieutenant his cousin, or more precisely his property, Achour refused to let us speak to him. Only he was allowed to: everyone else should simply listen and thank him for having a relative of this stature.

Touil wasn't really his cousin; they weren't related at all. Although they belonged to the same tribe, they'd only met in Tazmamart. But, like some intellectuals, Achour clung to a tribalist attitude that made him perniciously backward-looking and horribly bigoted.

Touil was a godsend for his block. Fate put him in Tazmamart so that lives might be saved. This was true for those in his block but also indirectly for those in ours; if we didn't benefit from his privileges ourselves, we could feel their repercussions. For many of us, a glimmer of hope had appeared and, most importantly, the guards' behaviour changed: they became more human. The reason for this was simple and could be summed up in a comment I heard one of them make: "The shame of it! Some of them are saved because they're married to Americans and others are killed because they're married to Moroccans. These days, you're a lot better off not being Moroccan!"

The words still echo in my mind because they reveal all the suffering of the developing world. Those who say they're fighting for human rights ought first to fight for human dignity and individual respect. Thanks to Touil's situation and the slight boost to the guards' nationalism, the toll of human lives in the eighties was not as high.

Behind his zeal to be the first to talk to his 'cousin', Achour concealed a morbid fear of seeing him make friends with one of us – you never know, he might have the audacity to send us something via the guards. After every visit, we could hear Achour striding up and down his cell in a rage, muttering under his breath. It put him in a very bad mood. He would go over every second of the encounter, every word uttered, every suspect noise. His imagination went into overdrive. He'd invent all kinds of unlikely scenarios that he'd end up brushing away with his hand. He'd stop for a moment, listen to the sounds of the building and he'd be off again, more furious than ever. Suddenly, for no apparent reason, he'd calm down and call out to me in a soft, brotherly voice. I never doubted that, in those moments, he was sincere and I was his brother. He wanted to ask me about something he'd remembered in the conversation with Touil, something he'd missed, a bit of news he hadn't heard or just a reference he wanted explained. In fact, he felt the pressure so intensely that he needed to be free of it or he would go mad. Achour was turning to the only person who might take pity on him. He knew I'd make something up, and even were I to tell him the truth he wouldn't have believed me. So I'd tell him what he wanted to hear. I reassured him. Yes, he made us miserable, but he was more miserable still. I couldn't abandon him; he was my cross to bear.

The Bourriquat brothers, whom I'll come back to later, were Achour's sworn enemies. He resented them for being civilians who had no business being in a military prison – as if there are categories in hell. Civilian or army, Jewish, Christian or Muslim, rich or poor, black or white, it's our hearts and our actions that will take us where we deserve to be. He resented the Bourriquats for constantly speaking in French when he could barely understand the language and for having no sympathy for him, not treating him with respect. But he also hated them because he enjoyed hating them.

One day, he suspected Bayazid Bourriquat of speaking to a guard and, in his deluded state, thought they'd been talking about him or perhaps the guard had given him something. The idea was intolerable to him. Taking advantage of a day when one of the soldiers (and not the kindest of them), Baghazi, was on his own and had agreed to leave the cell doors open while the meal was being served, allowing us to breathe, Achour rushed out and lunged at poor Bayazid – who was lying half-paralysed, motionless on the floor – and set about pummelling him with his fists. The other brothers, who were in equally bad shape, could not do a thing. We were rooted to the spot, stupefied. Never had we seen such a thing in Tazmamart: a physical assault! We were stunned. Who still had the strength to contemplate such heresy? Who had the courage to sacrifice a breath of fresh air? Who was mad enough to lay a hand on a dying man? In a word: Achour.

Although he was the oldest of us, physically he was the least afflicted. Perhaps that was why he thought he was king of us plague-ridden creatures.

We were worried about Baghazi's reaction; we would pay heavily for this. But here, too, the surprise matched the event.

The guard had served with Achour in the past and had known him a long time. Time and again, he'd shown his concern for him, and Achour, in his madness, thought Baghazi would cover for him – or, at worst, shut the doors for good and put an end to the fresh air, the little chats and his own personal torture, powerless as he was to control everything from his cell. This was no way to thank Baghazi, who'd done us an enormous favour, had risked his neck for us. He was pale with anger. Yet he'd spent long years with us, and he knew us all. At that time, the winds of change were blowing our way. In the outside world, especially abroad, people were beginning to talk about the prison. Terror was no longer as effective.

After a moment's reflection, the guard calmly walked over to Achour and ordered him back to his cell, which he double locked. Without saying a word to us, he left the block, locking the main door, and was gone, leaving our cells open. It would have been a fair and normal punishment for any of us, but how cruel for this particular prisoner! And what clearsightedness on the part of the illiterate guard. He took a malicious pleasure in prolonging the punishment. Since the other guards were on leave, he kept it up in the days that followed. For Achour, this was by far the most terrible time of his imprisonment. He'd made sworn enemies of the Bourriquats but also of Baghazi, who accused him of taking advantage of his kindness to try to sink him.

He didn't say another word to him until our release. The Bourriquats swallowed their pride, but they looked for every possible opportunity for revenge.

Block 2 also seemed to be avenging itself on those who'd temporarily abandoned it. It wasn't long before we suffered an enormous loss: our teacher, Abdellah Lafraoui. He was a *fqih* and son of a *fqih*; he knew the Qur'an by heart and had undertaken to teach it to us. This blessing filled a portion of our time, enabled us to learn and at the same time to escape. Lafraoui received scant reward for the service he'd done us. He'd become a casualty of the only radio we possessed. We'd managed to procure it through the negligence of the guards who'd searched Bouchaïb Skiba; they hadn't noticed the gold ring he wore on his finger. Miraculously the ring also survived the successive, more thorough searches every prisoner must undergo. We also owed the radio to man's greed, which sometimes impels him to overcome his deepest fears.

The guards were prone to fits of despair when their melancholy, mired in remorse, drove them to seek out a sympathetic ear to relieve their consciences. Not daring to open up to their fellow guards for fear of being falsely accused, they fell back on our passivity. They'd generally pour out their hearts to the convict who seemed to them the most discreet. One of these was Bouchaïb Skiba.

That day it was Corporal X who approached our comrade. He was one of the most brutal and most formidable guards, feared by everyone as he was said to be the commandant's informant. Standing by Skiba's door, he was recounting his trials and tribulations when he spotted the ring on his finger, glinting in the shadows of the cell.

"Oh," he said, "you've got a ring. How did you get that?"

Skiba leapt into the breach, replying, "The Lord saved it from the grasping hands of my tormentors so that it would reach you."

"Why me? What do you mean?"

"It's simple," Skiba went on. "I give it to you, you sell it and you bring me back half the money. I trust you; if Allah chose you to have it, it's because he knows you're a good man and you fear him."

"No! No!" cried the guard. "I can't do that! If I get caught, what will happen to me? They'll kill me! And anyway, if you don't have a receipt, I'll look like a thief!"

Skiba realised that if the man was scared of being accused, he was already imagining taking it. The timing was good; he'd been wanting to get rid of it for a while now. At the beginning, he'd been happy – he'd preserved his treasure. But as time went on, the ring had begun to mock him, had become an insult to his misery and the horror of this place. It linked him to the outside world, to life, to thwarted dreams, regret and remorse. He'd often considered throwing it down the toilet or in with the rubbish, yet each time he'd changed his mind.

Now he saw how he might kill two birds with one stone: he could rid himself of this symbol of his past and offer the whole block a window on the world.

"You know," our friend added, "you don't need to sell it. Take it – I'm giving it to you!"

"And what do you want in exchange?"

"Nothing but the Lord's blessing."

"That's not possible. You're giving it to me when you have nothing."

His greed was baffled. He couldn't get over the absurdity of the situation: a beggar giving alms. He threw up his hands and, from the depths of his unconscious burst the light of Allah's blessing, exactly as Skiba had been insisting throughout their conversation.

"All right, I'll take it, but I have to bring you something."

In a quiet, almost indifferent tone, Skiba answered, "The simplest, most practical thing would be a small radio."

The guard yelped, as if bitten by a snake.

"What? Are you mad? Do you want to get me killed? You want me to come and rot next to you?"

"Oh well, too bad then."

"Here, take your ring back. I don't want it."

"No, by Allah, I gave it to you. It's yours now and I don't want a thing for it."

Skiba went back inside his cell, leaving the corporal standing there, shifting his weight from one foot to the other, unsure what to do. Suddenly he slammed the door violently, checked the others were properly shut and stalked off, furious and confused.

Weeks and months passed with no sign of life from him. Skiba had rid himself of a jewel, an encumbrance to his serenity, and at the same time he'd flung a seed into the arid desert of a prison guard's heart. Perhaps one day it would rain and the seed would grow. Allah is great.

Rain fell on the master corporal's heart and the seed produced a transistor radio that he brought back one day when he was alone on duty under warrant officer first-class Frih. He was especially nervous: his gestures were abrupt, and he didn't stop grumbling. When he arrived outside Skiba's cell, he let out a barrage of insults; surprised, Skiba walked over to him. He pulled something surreptitiously from his pocket and put it in Skiba's hands, then banged the door shut and went to finish what he'd been doing.

Except the guard had taken such elaborate care to disguise his manoeuvre that he'd managed to arouse the suspicion of the warrant officer first-class, who'd been keeping an eye on him and rumbled his little ploy. The officer didn't dare act straightaway: he knew it was his word against his subordinate's. The latter might accuse him of his own transgression and, since he had the chief's ear, the initiative could backfire on him. He kept quiet, but this was only a postponement. At the next meal, he went straight to Lafraoui's cell – mistaking it for Skiba's – and accused him of taking something from his colleague. He searched the cell from top to bottom and found nothing. By now he was irate, so he imposed his favourite punishment. He stopped Lafraoui's water and food for several days, even though it was summer, and refused to let the rest of us quench his thirst. The episode ruined our comrade's health, which was already damaged by a chronic cough complicated by a fever that had lingered for years. He was transferred to the other block when the Africans arrived and came back to us sicker than ever. Not long after this, I dreamed of couscous. Lafraoui was dying. In a weak voice, he asked for a little water, since he was unable to move. In spite of our pleas, the warrant officer first-class would not let us help him. The guards were about to go on leave, but two of them had been confined to barracks in case Lafraoui died, which they resented fiercely. They dragged their feet until the warrant officer first-class left, then one of them said to the other, "Give him some water – just so long as he croaks!"

Which he did. Abdellah Lafraoui's soul went to his creator, and the guards went on leave, one fine day in the spring of 1983.

*

After this episode, Bouchaïb Skiba, who was acutely sensitive, refused to keep the offending radio. He hardly spoke, spending his time praying, practising yoga and 'communing with nature', as he called it. He had a huge appetite for culture, listened passionately to the novels I narrated and attentively followed my philosophy course (pitched at my own modest level), the theology lessons in particular. Most of my fellow inmates had some knowledge of other faiths, and we derived real pleasure from trying to understand them and especially from comparing them to Islam. There were vehement exchanges and stormy debates but never any real arguments, even when we got bogged down in minutiae. Skiba would listen carefully, sifting out what interested him and steering clear of any debate. He introduced us to yoga. We didn't know much about it, but we all contributed something. Then we'd each practise in our own way and exchange our impressions. As well as his yoga, Skiba was remarkable for his detachment from the world, which was inspired by Hindu stories. He also made many attempts to communicate from his cell with what he called in Arabic *Elkaoun*, literally 'everything that exists' – for me, 'the universal being'. He often abused his body, the better to master it. Did he succeed? I couldn't say, but he's still alive to tell us.

In a supreme act of detachment, Skiba decided to let us have the radio. The gesture was inconceivable in Tazmamart, especially in our wing. Who would be the chosen one? We decided to vote aloud, each person nominating someone else. The honour of opening the voting fell to Skiba, who declared for me. After that, the outcome was predictable. I received the magic box, having won a deafening majority. My job was to listen only to the news and report it to the others. We used a coded language we'd spent years devising, a language full of humour and derision.

One evening, when I was listening to the news on the national station, the speaker listed the names of people who'd been awarded the *Wissam* order of merit and I heard my mother's name. She was a tax inspector at the time. This knocked me sideways, but I pulled myself together very quickly. I had no right to hang on to such emotions. The main thing was that my mother was alive; I was glad, for her sake. My mind urgently needed to return to its cell, my universe.

The radio didn't last forever: the battery died, and we couldn't replace it. Playtime was over. The owl returned, taking the radio's place, but bringing what news? It had come for Mohammed Abdessadki, known as Manolo, who'd also returned from Block 1. The better conditions there couldn't have done him much good, and he fell ill.

Manolo was a veteran, originally from the Rif, who'd knocked about all over the country, criss-crossing the Algeria of protectorate days and working here and there in Spain doing all kinds of jobs before ending up in the ranks of the army and taking part in the civil war. Like all of life's adventurers, he knew when to show his joy and when to hide his tears. He was used to confronting difficult situations. The clearest memory I have of him goes back to the night he called out to us, sobbing, to tell us he was cold. He said he felt as if needles were going right through him, all over his body; he was crying. I was shocked because I didn't know you could cry from cold. Here was a man, a tough guy, who'd worked the most thankless jobs, who'd fought in the Spanish Civil War and lived through every kind of terrible ordeal, sobbing like a lost child because he was cold. Illness didn't make him cry – and nor did death, which he faced with dignity, like everyone else in Tazmamart. But he was crying from the cold.

Manolo was extremely weak and began to cough up blood. Internal bleeding, no doubt, but from where exactly? We couldn't say. His condition worsened as the days went on; he was vomiting more and more vile-smelling blackish blood. The guards were so disgusted by the stench they wouldn't open his cell door. They called on one of us to give him food and water; we'd use the opportunity to bring him what comfort we could. On his last evening, fate decreed that Rashid Lamine would be the one to spend the night with Manolo and help him through his last moments, hardly suspecting that his friend's death would pull him into the worst kind of nightmare.

Rashid was a friendly, talkative young man who'd definitely been spoiled as a child. That he was in the army at all had always amazed me; it was far easier to picture him working in a fabric shop than completing an army assault course. I couldn't have been more wrong! He was a warrant officer first-class in charge of air traffic control at the Kenitra base, Abounssi and Dghoughi's superior. Rashid couldn't bear the confinement and he told us he never slept, which wasn't quite true. He'd doze off and we'd tease him when he claimed not to have closed his eyes all night. As with our other comrades who said they didn't sleep at all, we'd sometimes call out to him in the middle of a story or a conversation and he wouldn't answer. Clearly, he was in the arms of Morpheus. And yet, at the end, he could tell you the whole story almost word for word.

Only when he was talking could Rashid forget his cell – he was a very poor listener – and the silence at night was torture to him. As soon as the sparrows announced the guards' arrival, Rashid would call out to someone and, like a drowning man coming up for air, he'd start talking. It had become a morning ritual: those who wanted to speak would wait for Rashid's opening gambit. His mental and psychological suffering was far worse than ours. Lack of sleep doubled the time he spent in his cell, since we'd deduct all the hours we spent sleeping from our sentences. He suffered, too, from not being able to talk as much as he wanted. There were other times, as well as during the night, when silence was compulsory: when the entire block was listening to a story, to Qur'anic teaching or to language lessons, or during other activities our community organised. All these tensions eventually wore him down. He felt his right side growing heavier and heavier. It was hard to move at all and finally he had to ask for a stick to be able to stand. The guards, who'd become more considerate, knew just how weak we were. They knew we weren't going to try anything. Even had we been up to it, a single one of them could easily have overpowered all of us survivors.

Since the guards now allowed us to help our sick comrades, they permitted Rashid, who was in bad shape himself, to support Manolo, who was on the verge of death. The warning signs had been with us for a few days: the owl had come and so had the portentous dreams that no one dared report for fear of causing the dying man to despair. Then came the smell, removing all doubt that someone was about to die – it would be a matter of hours at the very most. Manolo could no longer stand up. Sergeant Baghazi, who was on duty that evening, was the one to nominate Manolo's neighbour, Rashid, to help him during the night. This was a rare favour and Rashid could not refuse, in spite of his own poor health. So he went to spend the night with Manolo, who lay on his bunk, semi-conscious, haemorrhaging, continually spewing blood, which coagulated on his face, his neck and the rags he wore. A disgusting smell overlaid the stench of the cells and their inhabitants. When Rashid leaned over his patient to prop him up and tuck him in as best he could, he suddenly gagged, almost bringing up his food, so unbearable were the odours emanating from his friend's mouth. And yet, God knows we were used to bad smells! Overcoming his revulsion, Rashid covered him up as best he could and sat down by the concrete block that served as the sick man's bed so he'd be ready to assist him. In the middle of the night, he was woken by a raucous noise, a kind of angry snore followed by loud gurgling. He didn't have time to get to his feet to see what was going on. As if he were being strangled, Manolo was jerking up and down so violently that he was catapulted from his bunk and landed face down on top of Rashid, who could not move – paralysed by surprise, fear, disgust and the weight that was crushing him, suffocating him, by the smell of death that assaulted him, penetrated his senses and all the pores in his skin. He wanted to get away, to faint – even to die – but his brain and body would not obey him. Blood dripped onto his face, into his eyes and ears. He shut his mouth so he wouldn't swallow this liquid death. He wanted to retch, his whole being wanted to vomit, as if his life depended on it – but nothing. Hiccups rose from his stomach and stopped in his throat, unable to go up or down. He concentrated, every fibre in him strained to move his arms and push off this burden that was bent on dragging him with it into the torments of approaching death. He pushed with all the strength of his weak limbs; with everything he had, he prayed and he pushed. He called out to his mother and he pushed, he thought of his wife and his children and he pushed, he begged his brother for help and he pushed, he summoned all the fury he'd accumulated over nine years in Tazmamart and he pushed, he wanted to die and he pushed. Sisyphus lay flattened by his rock. The mountain no longer existed. Nothing existed beyond the rock and the curse that bore down with full force on his already failing health.

So he passed most of that night under the corpse – the night that wouldn't end, the night that decided his fate. When the guards arrived in the morning, Rashid was more dead than alive. Barely conscious, he was pulled out by his comrades who took him back to his cell. For several days he remained listless, no longer able to talk, paralysed down his right side, shuffling his feet and slurring his words, now and forever lugging the weight of that corpse – to the grave. He hauled it around for two more years before flinging it down in 1984, along with his own body, to be consumed by quicklime.

The arrival of the Bourriquat brothers in 1981 disrupted the life of the block. They were fascinating characters, by turns endearing and frightening, and they all had the same tone of voice yet were very different. Ali, the youngest, had set himself up as the brains of the gang – and perhaps the family – with a forceful personality and a definite gift for concealing his dominance. It would have made him a first-rate politician or the power behind the throne. His manipulative and calculating side was not innate; he'd inadvertently acquired it in the different circles he'd grown up in. He approached every undertaking as if his life depended on it and, like his older brothers, was always on the defensive.

Midhat was just as cunning as his brother, but his mind was less complex. He avoided direct confrontation, not out of cowardice or timidity but by disposition. As for Bayazid, I often wondered how he came to be with us. He had neither the stature nor the temperament of his brothers. He looked just like some middle-class shopkeeper who'd led a cushy life, his only concern to get rich. All three of them loved money, power, pleasure and especially good food – appetites that derived from their social status, or rather their family's: their mother was a cousin of Mohammed V and their father had been a French police officer during the protectorate. Tunisian first, then French and in the end Moroccan, their father was asked by the king to set up a secret service in a newly independent Morocco. So the Bourriquats lived in the orbit of the palace and some of them were said to socialise with princes.

Being his parents' favourite, Ali was without doubt the closest to the royal family.

The affair that led them to Tazmamart – and into several other secret places before that – was closely bound up with the money and intrigues of the palace. They have written about these themselves in the books they published on their release.

In Tazmamart, they put their talents at the service of their survival. They very quickly grasped the basic rules for coping with conditions in Block 2: joining the group and conforming to the regime we'd established for living and dying together. They gained an understanding of their fellow prisoners' personalities and adjusted their behaviour to each accordingly, but most importantly they brought fresh blood to the monotony of the prison. They had news: the death not only of Colonel M'hamed Ababou but of Captain Chellate, Akka and Mzireg, executed by firing squad after an escape bid the Bourriquats themselves had participated in, which was no doubt the reason they were here. They transported us to the worlds of business, politics and power, which up until then had been utterly opaque to us. They knew an impressive number of people and had the latest on all the rackets and alliances as well as the goings-on. They guided us through the labyrinths of power like huntsmen on their favourite reserve. They studded their accounts with anecdotes about such-and-such a person, affair or administration. Privy to all society gossip, they formed a living memory of contemporary Moroccan politics. We learned a great deal from them, some of which was true, some less so. But who cared? In Tazmamart, anything was good for the taking.

Ali and Midhat Bourriquat's great passion was Paris. They knew its every street and arrondissement, its cafés, restaurants and nightclubs, its cabarets, brothels, theatres and cinemas. They'd lived in the world's capital for many years and loved it above all else. They adored it so much they transmitted their passion to us. Together, we would stroll the streets of our Babylon for entire days, admiring the shops and the monuments, stopping in a famous café for a drink then carrying on our way, from marvel to marvel, surprise to surprise. Suddenly, turning a corner, the spell would be broken when an argument broke out between the two brothers over the location of a certain shop or café. The stroll would resume when, after our pleading, a compromise was reached.

Of course I had my preferences; how could I not? I liked to sit in a little bar on the Boulevard Saint-Michel or just on a bench in Saint-Germain, watching the passers-by, dreaming of freedom, awakening old demons that still plagued me from the days I imagined myself being a director, a journalist or a writer, the days when I dreamed of immortality.

In the end, we – and especially I – knew the streets of Paris as well as the Bourriquat brothers. Some of us preferred their passion for food. This gave rise to interminable discussions about different dishes in French, Moroccan and Tunisian cuisines. Fine dining and Turkish patisserie were the only solid links between the Bourriquats and the land of their grandparents. They could talk about food for hours on end. They weren't only gourmets but excellent cooks, and they were happy to share their knowledge.

Ten years is a long time. They exhausted their stock of

dreams and fantasies and had to wrestle with boredom and despair. Since, little by little, memory wanes and patience weakens, arguments over nothing became commonplace, both between the brothers and with others. Bayazid clung desperately to religion whereas his brothers, though tolerant, were honest enough to admit their lack of belief. This difference was scarcely a problem; each respected the others' convictions. We treated faith as what it's always been: a strictly personal matter.

The living conditions also got the better of their health. Bayazid was first to be affected. He could no longer walk and soon began to neglect himself, launching into unintelligible monologues. In lucid moments, he addressed his brothers with great insight. Sometimes, in the middle of his soliloquies, he'd catch a scrap of conversation and join in the discussion as if nothing were amiss. The proximity and affection of his brothers saved him from going mad. Much later, it was Midhat's turn to fall apart. He lost the use of his feet and did what his brother had done, sleeping near the door so he could reach his food and crawl to the toilet. Ali looked after them, of course, cleaned their cells and their clothes and did their 'washing up', but nothing could be taken for granted; the guards might change their minds at any moment and stop him going into his brothers' cells. Achour's attack on Bayazid, who was unable to move, was the last straw. They declared their fierce hatred of Achour and swore to get even. They knew how to hold a grudge.

The brothers were released a few weeks after us, which was as long as it took to negotiate their silence; these men knew too much.

Before Tazmamart, they'd come across warrant officer first-class Akka at so-called 'point M', where they'd been held prisoner. Even at the time, wild rumours were circulating about the adventures of this colossus. Some were true and some were born of the imagination of a people who, in their childish need for the fantastical and extraordinary, seek an outlet for their woes.

One story went that, during the coup d'état, an armed man accompanied by cadets had entered the wing of the palace where the king's concubines lived. Frightened to death, the women had huddled in a corner, clinging to each other. He'd approached them, suddenly roaring with laughter, then knelt down next to one of the women, wedging the barrel of his gun against her crotch and said, "Isn't this the king's favourite?"

Terrified, she was trembling all over when a giant appeared behind him and sent him flying with one kick, bellowing in Berber, "Aren't you ashamed to attack women, you coward? Get out of here or I'll kill you!"

The men cleared off and the giant left the room after making sure no one had been left behind. The women reported the incident and, based on the descriptions they gave, the investigators identified Akka. A legend had grown up around this enigmatic figure, made famous by his unconditional devotion to his master. In the early days of our incarceration, when we were still in Kenitra, the king – according to hearsay – had asked for him. And it was true that, one evening, the gendarmes had taken him away, cuffed and blindfolded. He had disappeared for part of the night and was then brought back to his cell. The next day, a rumour went around that he had met the king. Akka remained tight-lipped about the interlude but rumour was less discreet. It was said that, during the conversation, the king had asked for the name of the man who had insulted his concubine, and promised him his freedom in exchange. Apparently, Akka had denied knowing the culprit's name.

We were agreed on the first part of the story and on Akka's intervention, less so on the identity of the brute who'd abused the women, although rumour pointed to Achour. I couldn't say how the Bourriquat brothers found this out but, when we were transferred to Ahermoumou before our release, they asked to see someone in charge and told him the whole story.

The consequences were immediate. After we were released, Achour was transferred with Raiss, his alter-ego from the other block, to Kenitra's civilian prison. They were not included in the royal pardon. Were it not for the vigorous intervention of human rights groups, he would be there still.

Tazmamart was home to animals, too. First, there was Commandant Elkadi's ewe. She was a scrawny beast that our chief must have bought cheaply in the local souk. The safest place to keep her was obviously the prison yard, so she became our neighbour. She had the advantage of being in the sun and the open air, enjoying good grass. The soldiers' rural backgrounds meant they treated her properly. Everyone lavished attention on our guest, who proved to be fertile. In every litter she delivered at least two but often four lambs. Six months later, the commandant would task his men with taking the lambs to the souk to sell them. The ewe spent some years like this, within our walls. If she didn't make Elkadi rich, she undoubtedly made the guards happy; they looked on her with affection, as a symbol of abundance, and yet they never asked themselves about the misery that festered not far from this ewe.

One day, she disappeared. We were worried and asked the guards what had happened; they answered sadly that the chief had sold her.

As if to drive the ghosts from this place of death, the colonel didn't leave the yard empty. Very quickly he restocked it, but this time with a dog. Rumour had it that she was an old mongrel the chief wanted rid of. He parked her in the same place as the fertile ewe, but she wasn't as popular with the guards since she produced neither milk nor lambs. They fed her with the leftovers from the barracks and complained about her fussiness, since she wouldn't eat certain foods. They called her the colonel's spoilt bitch.

One day, we heard them grumbling that she'd refused to eat some buttered bread. We were appalled. It had been years since we'd seen butter anywhere except in our dreams and here they were throwing it to the commandant's old dog who, what's more, turned up her nose!

Another time, she made an appearance in our wing. She'd never come into a prison block before that holiday and, when she arrived in front of ours, she stood there for a long while, as if hesitating. What stopped her coming near the buildings? Did she see ghosts, like the guards? No one will ever know. Finally, she decided to come in. She went round the cells one by one, pausing for a moment in front of each door, omitting none. Then she left and never came back. No doubt her fine sense of smell did not appreciate her wretched neighbours' stench.

Death, dark thoughts, anguish… sometimes it's in the worst moments, when morale is lowest, when hope becomes suffering and the darkness is total, that "light shines from the darkest corner". A few months had gone by since the radio incident and it had almost been forgotten when one day Bendourou, who was usually enveloped in his exaggerated asceticism and refused to have anything to do with us, asked to speak. An astonished silence fell. We were all ears, curious to know what this rebel would reveal.

"Skiba!" he called. "Did you really swap your ring for a radio?"

"I did," Skiba answered.

"Then listen, everyone. I have some gold, a lot of gold. And as you know, the guards don't like me. So I'm going to entrust it to one of you, so you can try to trade it."

We were speechless. A lot of gold! How was this possible? Had the captain lost his mind?

"Where did you get this gold?" someone asked.

"Never mind about that! You'll see. I'm going to send it through the walls to Skiba. Since he already has a contact with one of them, he can ask him again."

The whole building was astir, trying to work out the best way for the treasure to reach its destination. Perching on their water pitchers, comrades struggled to convey the precious cargo, directed by their neighbour's voice. The journey took time; it was an escape from our daily life, our boredom and misery.

When the packet finally reached its destination, Bendourou addressed his chosen partner, "Listen, I know the value of this gold, don't try conning me, it's worth millions."

Skiba, usually the soul of discretion, was helpless with laughter. He panted breathlessly, "They're teeth!"

We were dumbstruck. What did he mean, *teeth*? We had to know.

"They're teeth, crowns and bridges, in gold and platinum!"

Of course: like the rest of us, the ex-captain was losing his teeth, but he'd kept back those that were valuable. Once he was sure that Skiba's ring had brought in something decent, he was considering a trade of his own. We all laughed heartily; everyone made jokes. The angrier, more impatient and more abusive Bendourou became, the more we laughed.

When the general hilarity died down, we began to reflect on the best way to proceed, knowing that the presence of this treasure wouldn't scare the guards: since we were proposing to exchange teeth that had come from one of us, they weren't likely to be accused of bringing them in.

All our attempts were in vain. None of the guards would agree to the deal, least of all the corporal. Bendourou took back his property and guarded it jealously until he died. I'd often hear him grumbling in his cell, accusing us of not wanting to trade his millions; we were just a bunch of jealous, envious men.

To kill time, some of us talked, others told stories, often about their lives, and others simply made them up. It didn't matter; what was important was to escape from reality, from madness and pain. So I couldn't say what's true and what isn't in my accounts of my comrades' lives before Tazmamart. As to what happened inside, God is my witness.

Boujemâa Azendour was a friend who graduated in the same year as me; he was my cellmate and my confidant. He had been to the Royal Military Academy and graduated an officer. This was an act of revenge on life and on his father, who had served in the French colonial army as a soldier, a rank that was converted into corporal in the Moroccan army. With the height and build of a giant – and a prophet's beard to match – Boujemâa's father was chosen to be the standard-bearer in passing-out parades and official ceremonies.

As a young recruit deployed with troops going to Indo-china, he had entrusted his wife and their two children – a little girl and a little boy, Boujemâa – to his own elderly father, who was half-blind, stubborn, stocky and as strong as Hercules. After their mother died and in the absence of their father, the children grew up under the wing of this self-serving, sour-tempered old man.

For him, the little ones were manna from heaven: unpaid labour. The girl took care of the housework while the boy looked after the two cows and three goats that comprised the family's livestock. At harvest time, when the whole tribe gathered for the collective labour known as the *touiza*, it was the kids who represented the family and did the work that was his responsibility.

The *touiza* was originally a Berber institution and went back to Morocco's tribal system. The tribal council would assemble to identify families that didn't have the physical or financial capability to gather their crops or reap their harvest. Then all the families would designate a young man or boy to work in the fields and a young woman or girl to cook and serve the meals.

The old man kept putting his grandchildren forward. It cost him nothing and earned him a certain respect within the tribe. The children were glad, too, as it meant getting away from their grandfather and they enjoyed the atmosphere of celebration on *touiza* days, when everyone was happy and light-hearted. It was all laughter, singing and joking on those memorable days. Their tribe, the Maghraoua, was the only one in the kingdom whose people spoke Berber but sang in Arabic.

For some reason or other – certainly not self-respect – the grandfather refused the community's help. He laboured, reaped and harvested alone, in spite of his disability.

His grandchildren weren't just free labour; they also represented a substantial source of revenue. He claimed the cost of food and board from their father, who was only too happy to pay, relieved to have found someone to look after his offspring – first while he was in Indochina and then upon his return, when he remarried and established a new household. His children only came to know him through rare, brief visits to their former home. He was always away when, later on, serious incidents pitted Boujemâa against his grandfather.

The old man decided to marry off the girl when she was twelve (which was a normal age for country girls to marry at the time) to a man forty years her senior, because he had a fine herd and several acres of good arable land. Since the bride price was substantial, the old man had no qualms about trading her. Her status changed from little-girl-slave to child-mother-slave. Her brother's recriminations fell on deaf ears. To oppose his rapacious grandfather, all the little ten-year-old had was anger and tears. His sister left and he never saw her again.

This decision sparked Boujemâa's rebellion. Many times he had begged his grandfather to let him go to school, but the response, always the same, was expressed in the man's violence: a good thrashing, or those random, lunging swipes of which only the blind are capable. Yet the boy, who watched his neighbours set off on the road to school, began to dream, and the institution only grew in his imagination. Magic emanated from the word 'school' – the key that opened the doors of the future, the roads to the city he'd heard so much about and, most of all, that promised deliverance from the rule of the despot who enslaved him.

One morning, he took the animals out as usual and led them to pasture in the forest. He knew the best places, where the village shepherds would meet. The sun was just brimming on the horizon when he caught up with a friend and asked him to tend his animals for the day.

"Where are you going?" the friend asked.

"To school," he replied.

"You're mad! Your grandfather will kill you! And anyway, the school's fifteen kilometres from here!"

"Look after my animals, please."

"All right, if that's what you want."

Boujemâa ran off, sprinted the fifteen kilometres as if in a dream, and found himself by the gate of the still-deserted school. He decided to sit and wait. The pupils arrived in small groups carrying their satchels. Some of them wore smocks that were all alike. He thought that perhaps those children were more advanced than the others. *One day I'll wear a long shirt and I'll know a lot too.* The school bell interrupted his reverie. *What's that strange noise? It sounds like a giant flute.* The pupils rushed into the yard through the gate, which had just opened. Daunted, he went closer, watching them run all over the place chirping like sparrows. Seizing his moment, he slipped inside and went to hide behind a tree trunk. He felt lost. What should he do? Where should he go? Who should he talk to? And all that noise… Suddenly, the bell rang again. He was stunned; this time the sound was right beside him. Then everything went quiet. The children stopped talking and went to line up in front of a classroom. A man in European clothes with a long stick in his hand came out of the room and glanced severely at the schoolchildren. Not a murmur from the ranks. Boujemâa felt himself weaken, his knees trembled, he wanted to run away but it was too late, the school gate had already closed. He wanted to melt into the tree trunk. The pupils began to go in. He had to make a decision. It was no good; he couldn't stay there rooted to the spot until school was out. He took his courage in both hands and threw himself into the room just as the last pupil went in the door.

The others were all standing in front of their desks. He started to panic, then noticed an empty place in the back row. He weaved his way towards it and sat down, making himself as inconspicuous as possible. The teacher didn't notice him but the rest of the class did, and whispered questions came from all sides. The teacher motioned them to sit down, but the whispering grew louder and everyone turned around to look at the intruder. Poor Boujemâa looked like a bird that had fallen out of its nest.

The teacher's voice rose sharply, silencing the commotion, "What's going on?"

"A new boy, sir."

"What? Where is he? Why wasn't I told? Who are you, my boy? What's your name? Where have you come from?"

Boujemâa was terrified. He looked about him like an animal caught in a trap. His anxiety intensified as the man approached. But the teacher quickly noticed his distress. He stopped and asked in a kinder voice, "Do you speak French, my boy?"

Nothing.

"Do you speak Arabic?"

Still nothing. No response at all.

"Berber, perhaps?"

He saw a gleam of hope in the boy's eyes. He went on in Berber.

"Who are you?"

"Boujemâa," he said in a strangled voice.

"What are you doing here?"

"I came to school."

"Why?"

"To read."

"To read what?"

"Just to read."

"Do you know how to read?"

"No, I've never been to school."

"Have you registered?"

He fell silent again and hung his head.

"All right, then."

The master walked over to a cupboard and pulled out an exercise book, a pencil and a slate. He handed them to Boujemâa and asked him to sit down in the first-year row.

"We'll do your registration with the headmaster later."

In the classroom, each row corresponded to a level up to primary school certificate. Boujemâa found himself in the little kids' row. But no matter! At last he was at school – ragged, lice-ridden, barefoot, but at school.

At midday, most of the schoolchildren went home to have lunch, others nibbled at sandwiches before his famished eyes, but that didn't matter. He stood there, in front of the school, feeling exhilarated. Too bad if he didn't have a satchel, that was a detail. And his grandfather would accept it in the end – he'd have to. Anyway, he wouldn't give up the fight, wouldn't be told what to do, like his sister. He was a man. He'd get a letter written to his father; maybe, for once, he would understand and intervene. This was so important.

At two o'clock, he went back to class and at five, as soon as school was over, he raced home, covering the fifteen kilometres in record time. Alas, not quickly enough to catch the boy who was looking after his animals. The latter, fearing for his life, had gone back to the village and returned the livestock to Boujemâa's grandfather. Unable to account for Boujemâa's absence, he told the old man about the school, which caused an explosion of fury and incomprehension.

"School!" he yelled. "Who in our family ever went to school? That's all I need! And who's going to look after my cows? Ah, that useless boy, he's got it coming. I'll skin his hide with my stick, he'll see!"

Boujemâa found the old man seething with rage in the doorway. As soon as he heard Boujemâa's footsteps, the grandfather began to rant and bellow, since he was incapable of running after him.

"You ungrateful little brat! How can you think of going to school when I brought you up, fed you, taught you to look after cows? I gave you a bed in my house and you dare to betray me."

The boy knew there was no hope and that if he went inside, he risked being beaten to death. Wisely he retreated and went to huddle in a sheltered corner; perhaps the night would soften his tormentor's heart.

The next day, Boujemâa went to school without going back to the house. On the way, he ate fruit that he picked in the forest. This venture lasted a few days. One fine morning, his grandfather burst into the schoolyard shouting, hurling abuse and demanding his grandson be returned to him. The pupils rushed to the windows, the teacher ran outside and, alerted by the shouting, the headmaster appeared with the caretaker. Never had the little school known such drama. It took a while to find out what all the shouting was about and what this madman wanted. Those in authority tried to reason with him, explaining how school could benefit him as well as the child. It was no use. He wouldn't listen to anyone and carried on shouting.

The teacher, an Algerian from Kabylia, was tall, with a commanding presence. He started shouting louder than the old man and ordered him to leave the school grounds immediately or he'd have the gendarmes called. He argued that education was compulsory now and he had no right to deprive his grandson of knowledge. Realising he would not get his way, the old man left, cursing, and immediately went to lodge a complaint with the caid.* He was sent away again with the same arguments. For the first time in his life, the grandfather felt helpless – even more so than on the day he'd begun to lose his sight. He was adjusting to blindness but could not tolerate this insurrection, sparked by a snot-nosed kid. In his head, hatred jostled with rage and this powerlessness. He felt betrayed, defeated and humiliated. He wanted to get even. At home, he went over to the tree trunk propping up the roof of the adobe house and tried to fell it, pushing it with all his might until it gave way and pulled part of the structure down with it. The old man lay on the ground, half-buried in rubble. The neighbours came rushing over, pulled

* The local representative of the state's authority.

him out and sent for his grandson to come to look after him. Boujemâa arrived at a run and had to take care of his relative. What the latter hadn't been able to achieve by force, he thought he could effect by cunning. He was wrong.

The very next day, Boujemâa was on the road to school again. The old man begged, pretended he was dying, tried every trick his twisted mind could come up with; nothing could sway the boy. Then he decided he'd wear him down. He accepted God's command, he said, but carried on by stealth. As for Boujemâa, his education was barely interrupted, and now, after his grandfather's stick-wielding intervention, he had the benefit of everyone's sympathy. Very quickly he learned to read, write and count. He moved from the first row to the second, then to the third, doing so well that, after three years, he passed his school certificate.

Boujemâa was accepted at secondary school with honours, which earned him a bursary for boarding in Taza. At last, he'd made it! The world was his oyster, nothing could stop him now. He didn't tell his grandfather until the day he was due to leave. He was dreading a violent scene but, amazingly, the old man didn't say a word. He had learned that his grandson was a great success and that he had to leave to carry on with his education. He'd got the measure of the force driving his ward and knew that he himself was too weak now; he'd given up, or perhaps a glimmer of understanding had enlightened his turbulent spirit. They say light sometimes bursts from the darkest corners. Throughout his grandson's secondary education and until his own last breath, he never again gave him an order and only ever called him 'Sidi' Boujemâa.

Taza didn't yet have a lycée. When he had finished the first part of secondary school, Boujemâa had to find somewhere else to study. He wrote to his father, who was garrisoned in Marrakech, and, for the first time in his life, went to live with him, and could begin to get to know him. He enrolled in a lycée and came to live in the southern capital, where he encountered a different style of living, a different way of thinking and entirely different habits.

In the very first year he was there, his father was posted to a village that had no lycée. The issue of education reared its head again, and again fate ordained that school won out: a friend of his father's, a sergeant who'd risen from the ranks and was also illiterate, suggested that Boujemâa live with him until his baccalaureate exam. This man was childless and had a quasi-religious respect for the educated, 'the learned', as he called them. At last Boujemâa came to know the affection and tenderness he'd so badly missed and had a taste of that family life he'd only ever heard about. This good man and his wife fussed over him, spoiled him and mothered him. When he talked about this time in his life, his eyes would fill with tears. In the year that led up to his exam, his adoptive father came to his room every night after his military duties, made him coffee, sat down beside him to watch him work, without a word, and stayed there. When Boujemâa wanted to recite a lesson, the sergeant would take up the book or exercise book authoritatively and say, "Go on, recite, I'm listening."

As he recited, the sergeant would nod his head with a knowing look. If Boujemâa tripped up, he'd clear his throat and say, "I'm not sure that's correct; have a look, check."

The strangest thing was that he was often right. The explanation was simple: noting some hesitation or a slightly altered tone, the illiterate sergeant realised Boujemâa had made a mistake.

Thanks to this family, Boujemâa sat his baccalaureate in the best possible circumstances and sailed through. That day, his guardians wept as if they themselves, or a child of theirs, had succeeded. It was their revenge on illiteracy.

Equipped with his diploma, Boujemâa sat the entrance exam for the Royal Military Academy, which he passed. After two years' study, he became an officer. Now he was part of the army his father had served his whole life, for the sake of which he'd abandoned him and his sister. When his father saw him in his brand-new uniform, he congratulated him as if he were a stranger, without looking him in the eye. He felt no pride. In no way could he participate in his son's success, which was thanks to the boy's willpower alone.

In Tazmamart, Boujemâa lived as he always had, with dignity and courage. He ignored petty problems and the hassles of everyday life. He was immune to them. He fell ill, but we never knew what from. He didn't complain; his death was almost a surprise. Had the barefoot shepherd boy's determination deserted him? This little Berber who sang in Arabic had just one dream in life: to be able one day to cuddle his sister, spoil her, give her back a tiny bit of that stolen childhood, those thwarted dreams. Children are children because our suffering protects them like a prayer.

I could barely even have sketched the portrait of Abdeslam Haifi before Tazmamart. He had served a year longer than me, so was my 'elder'. When he realised the desperateness of our situation, he turned his back on reality and took refuge in a world of hatred and spite. It's a miracle he survived so long. He sank into a mild kind of madness, spending his days reciting a litany of abuse against the entire planet, a diatribe only interrupted by sleep. He insulted people we knew and people we didn't, a lot of well-known figures but no one from the cell block.

He stood out right from the start because of a bizarre performance. When the guards opened his cell door to give him his ration of starch, he took to his heels, hurtled down the corridor and emerged outside in the yard. The element of surprise was highly effective. Once they'd recovered from the shock, the guards set off in pursuit and caught him in the yard, where he was running round in circles, unable to go any further. Furious, they beat him and brought him back to his cell, punching him all the while. For a long time afterwards, the guards would curse whenever they opened Haifi's cell. Needless to say, they left him without food for many days. In this incident, the most vicious of them was warrant officer first-class Ben Driss. When I pointed out to Frih, the head guard in our block, that their reaction was disproportionate, given that there was no chance of Haifi escaping, he answered very angrily that the sentries had orders to shoot anyone coming out of the cell blocks and that, on that day, the guards had nearly been gunned down at the same time as Haifi.

Abdeslam Haifi fell ill at the beginning of the eighties: he was suddenly unable to move. The guards allowed one of us to take him his food and try to help him while they served the others their meal. He didn't die straightaway; his death throes were endless. And he went on insulting people until his last breath. When he died, the guards told us to take him out into the corridor, since they refused to go into the cells anymore, appalled by the stench and fearful of infection. But how could they have caught anything in that place where even germs couldn't have survived? It was a gruesome sight. Haifi was now only a few dozen inches long: his legs, bent double, were stuck to his chest, he had hardly an ounce of flesh left on him and what flesh there was, the maggots had started on. One of the guards picked him up in one hand like a bag and took him to his last bath – of quicklime. He left behind him thousands of cockroaches; the cell was infested with them. They were everywhere. Not an inch of the ceiling, walls or ground wasn't covered in swarming cockroaches, all orphans now.

The next day, the guards arrived with an insecticide pump. They explained that some desert locust control experts had given it to them, advising that they put on gas masks to use it. Since they didn't have any, they made it clear without the least scruple that we would be the ones to operate it. To their minds, we had nothing left to lose. We agreed; perhaps we shared their view. After spraying the unfortunate cockroaches with the lethal solution and closing the door, we left the poison to do its work. The next day, we were still alive whereas the cockroaches had been exterminated. It was with shovel and wheelbarrow that the guards rid us of that pest.

*

In 1985, death ran out of breath. That was the first year no one died – unhappily, the respite would be brief. We were worn out, broken, done for, no longer of interest to death. Our skin had wizened on our misshapen skeletons; we walked oddly, as if at any moment we might disintegrate. Our faces were those of dead men: wild eyes framed by tufts of dirty, bushy hair, like trophies impaled on stakes in cannibal villages.

Our brains couldn't keep up: we'd lost our power of concentration, the sharpness of our memory, the force of our imagination and the liveliness of our minds. All this was due to the living conditions, the privations, the emotional shocks and – we learned later, courtesy of Touil – the lack of oxygen. In fact, among the medicines his wife sent him were pills to help oxygenate the brain. At that time, my comrades and even the guards told me that I kept rocking my head backwards and forwards in an automatic, unconscious movement. So I started paying attention to it, careful attention, which was all the more difficult in that I didn't realise I was doing it. In the end, I managed to control these spasmodic movements by remaining hyper-vigilant.

We would spend the winter prostrate on our concrete benches, drowning in a whirligig of dreams and memories that were splintered, ragged, flickering and fading. Now our only thought was of getting through the present moment, of surviving; we no longer had any expectations at all. We were exhausted, worn out, just dragging ourselves towards the end with as much dignity as we could muster. We had nothing more to say to one another, nothing to tell and, in any case, we could no longer even listen or stay alert; our ability to pay attention was close to zero.

When summer came, we'd haul ourselves towards the diagonal, still trying to cling to life. We were not giving up, we kept fighting, where there's life… Even on the day the guards arrived in the yard and spent all morning digging holes. We could hear them; what were they doing now? We were intrigued, anxious and, above all, curious. At the end of the third day, they stopped. The prisoner whose cell was opposite the door saw what was happening and didn't want to worry us but, when we pressed him, he told us: they were digging holes along the wall, each the length of a man. Counting them, we deduced that this was the number of surviving prisoners in both blocks. The conclusion was obvious. The guards later admitted that these holes were indeed destined for us. But the plan was changed. Why? We learned that, after the publication of Gilles Perrault's book *Notre ami le roi* and the extraordinary work of Christine Daure-Serfaty, international pressure had become such that the regime eventually had to yield. In the first instance, they gave up the idea of killing us; next, they admitted our existence to the world, and finally the idea of releasing us began to take hold. The tenacity, stubbornness and faith of one woman defeated the will of a state to hide its true face.

Our daily round continued, though the guards almost never closed the doors now; they had nothing to fear from the walking skeletons we'd become. The days became harder and harder physically, we were weaker and weaker mentally, and yet Tazmamart was less and less avid for death. Boujemâa died in 1986 and Haifi three years later. Those were the three years we spent romping through the streets of Paris in our fantasies with the Bourriquat brothers. That's what kept us connected to life.

Then, one day, two nurses turned up, asked about the state of our health and distributed a few strips of aspirin and a magic powder for stomach cramps. It was nothing, but our desiccated skulls derived enormous benefit from it. We could feel our spirits begin to lift. A soft breeze from the open sea caressed our foreheads, whistling a joyous air of freedom.

Twenty years earlier, before the hapless adventure that would lead us to Tazmamart prison, we were living peacefully, dozing in the humdrum lethargy of barracks life at Ahermoumou. We were young, careless and naive. Fresh from the Royal Military Academy, we saw ourselves as great strategic thinkers of the future. It wasn't long before we became disenchanted. Reality arrived in the form of embittered ex-officers who, along with their illusions, had lost that fire that drives a person to rattle the cages of habit and routine, avoid the pitfalls of the easy life and grasp the flame of ambition.

Among those officers there was one who made a lifelong impression on me; my destiny was linked with his until death did us part.

He'd showed up in full armour, astride his white charger, impaling all the windmills before him; this noble knight had the rank of captain and came from the Royal Gendarmerie, where it seemed his antiquated notions were not appreciated. He landed in my battalion and was made its commander. On the very first day, he sent round a memo demanding a meeting of joint chiefs of staff. This was unheard of. What meeting? What joint chiefs of staff? We were only really vague supervisors charged with delivering lessons programmed by the director of studies, and he was just a general supervisor. The titles 'section leader', 'company commander', 'battalion commander' were just words on a flow chart copied from the set-up a cadet would encounter when he left and joined the army proper.

This was the beginning of my journey with the man who would inhabit the cell next to mine in Block 2 in Tazmamart. Powerfully built with broad shoulders, a broken nose, square jaw and docker's hands, Bendourou's physique was impressive, but his intelligence and common sense were less than dazzling. He always missed the point. 'Friendship', 'respect', 'generosity', even 'love' were hollow words to him. And yet some goodness lay hidden in his innermost soul and surfaced every time he mentioned his daughter. Those were the only moments when flashes of humanity gleamed in his eyes. On the other hand, his face would become a mask as soon as he mentioned his son. He struck me as having had a brutal upbringing, and consequently he unleashed all that pent-up aggression onto his boy.

This went for the soldiers under his command, too, and was the first cause of disagreement between us. I was a company commander in his battalion, and I wouldn't stand for my men being abused. I was against arrests with pay deducted, which he would hand out at will. During battle fitness drills, he'd march out in front and keep up a fast pace, leaving stragglers behind all the way along. I used to make it a point of honour to bring back my full unit, urging the stronger ones to help the weaker, which he would not permit.

Fate made us neighbours in prison, condemning us to live pent up together. The first year passed without too much trouble. When we told stories, he would feign sleep while not missing a word. When we began Qur'anic lessons, he joined the group and began learning with us. We were only able to memorise an eighth of a verse per day at first. At the end of a few verses, like many of us, he would lose his place, because we had to learn the daily eighth as well as going over the preceding verses so we didn't forget them. Bendourou needed me to help him revise his verses and carry on learning at his pace. As I was his nearest neighbour, I was the only one who could help him. The others would certainly have refused anyway, given his arrogance and his way of claiming things as his due or our duty. I wasn't too bothered by this; I was only giving back what had been given so generously to me. And besides, these were my good deeds: I helped him the same way I supported Achour and Dghoughi.

The day he reached his limit, he stopped. It was no use my asking if he needed help; he wouldn't answer. He no longer responded to anyone. He thought he was entrusted with a God-given mission that commanded him to fast, pray and recite the Qur'an at all hours. The rest of us miserable sinners no longer deserved a place in his universe.

He would store his daily food allowance to eat at night; in winter it would be frozen, in summer slightly rancid. He kept up this regime to the end. In fact, he only fasted this way because he preferred to eat our measly ration as one vaguely consistent meal.

When human beings behave irrationally, they're hiding behind beliefs, ideologies or rituals they believe are superior.

One day I advised him not to leave his food to go off, arguing that it might backfire on him in the end. He called me Satan, and said I was jealous and wanted to stop him from entering paradise. Another cause of our falling out was his habit, when he wasn't sleeping, of reciting the Qur'an under his breath in a monotone, which was like the constant hum of an engine. Many times I begged him to stop. In vain. It only encouraged him to chant louder. When I insisted, he shouted, "Shut up, Satan!"

One evening, soon after the six o'clock meal, he began to mutter in his usual way. I asked him sharply to be quiet. He didn't answer. I cursed him. He said nothing for a moment, then called out, "You dare to insult me, you bastard. You know, and everyone here and outside knows, you're just a bastard! Your father officially disowned you in front of the whole country!"

With this insult he'd just declared open warfare, for this man – who pretended to be elsewhere, so devoted was he to religious life and prayer – of course missed nothing of what went on in the prison. One practice that every single one of us had adopted was to listen carefully to everything everyone recounted about their lives, their pasts and their adventures; we'd pick up on anything that one day, should an argument break out, could be used to hurt them. We'd make a note of each man's weak points and strong suits. I was no exception to the rule. I'd told my life story, including an exchange which had been reported back to me in the early days, when we were in Kenitra: my father, who was close to the king, was asked this question by his ruler after the events at Skhirat, "So, BineBine, are you happy about what your son's done?"

My father, presumably in self-defence, said, "Majesty, I do not recognise this individual. A traitor to the king cannot be my son!"

The response must have pleased the monarch, since he never mentioned the subject again. And now the story had been thrown back in my face, with the obvious intention to wound me deeply. Captain Bendourou had never confided in anyone. He believed his silence and reserve shielded him from the murderous attacks we could launch. He hadn't counted on the inspiration of Satan, ever on the prowl for situations like this, and on my memory, which that day proved Machiavellian. I'd known for years that confrontation with him was inevitable. So I'd planned my tactics in minute detail. I was convinced my adversary was a giant with feet of clay. I knew when and how to strike. But first I had to warm him up, push him to such a degree of exasperation that he'd be incapable of reasoning.

The argument lasted the whole night, until the guards arrived the next morning. In this type of contest, the loser was the one who fell silent first. In the middle of the night, at the height of the argument, my tone cold, almost calm, I said, "Cuckold!"

He didn't pick up on the reference immediately. I shouted out the word again three or four times, coolly enough to perturb him. When I felt he was slightly puzzled and was certain he would hear me, I said, "Cuckold, you're the father of a bastard."

And I waited a beat. He was stunned. I could tell he'd taken the bait and was torn between anger and doubt, but sufficiently intrigued that I could make my move before he'd recovered. I went on, sounding almost friendly, "Tell me, when we were in Kenitra prison, your wife definitely came to the hospital and you slept with her. If you've forgotten, it was on such-and-such a date, wasn't it?"

Astounded by the accuracy of my information, he replied with a barely audible 'yes'. I continued more loudly (I had to drive home my advantage), "She gave birth to a baby on such-and-such a date, didn't she?"

Again, the accuracy floored him. Then, like the lash of a whip, "Can you explain why there are exactly nine months minus ten days between those two dates, when a normal pregnancy is exactly nine months?"

My calculations were diabolically precise. Pregnancy does not obey the rules of mathematics, of course – it's usually nine months give or take a few days – but I made sure not to tell him that. I didn't give him time to think. I wanted him obsessed with the calculations, unable to think about anything else. As soon as he saw what I was getting at, I changed the subject and let out a volley of insults aimed at various weak points, so that he couldn't go back to his sums. But he'd already been wrong-footed.

In the morning, before the guards arrived, he went quiet; I carried on for a while, savouring my victory. It was the longest, most brutal and cruellest argument that took place within the walls of Block 2. My first and last battle. I was not proud of myself.

When the guards had gone, Bendourou called out to resume hostilities, but it was over. I'd had enough and, above all, I didn't want to give him the chance to come back in.

A few days later, he called me and asked in a hesitant voice, "Are you sure you got those calculations right? You couldn't be mistaken?"

How could I tell him that the calculations meant nothing,

that their only significance was to do with where he was psychologically at that point in the argument?

When Bendourou fell ill, I did everything in my power to make up for the way I'd behaved. It was towards the end of our incarceration and the guards were more relaxed; they let me go and sweep his cell. I washed his pots and clothes while he cursed me and accused me of stealing his things. No one wanted to help him now, because of how he was. He had no obvious sign of illness, but he was fading away; he'd become so weak he couldn't get up, victim to the draconian regime he'd imposed on his body.

It was the beginning of spring and, little by little, we were coming out of our enforced hibernation. This colossus had survived the trials of winter, but could he overcome the doubt that haunted him? Could he, having made it through the storm, land on the shores of deliverance, which already beckoned? Could he stave off Tazmamart's fate, while eighteen long years of misery and horror bore down on him? Could he refute the predictions of the macabre seer who came each evening to sing its litany of despair? Finally, could he hold on to the hope that those two poor nurses would have the magic potion that would save him? That they weren't just going through the motions?

So we waited…

Bendourou died on 8 May 1991, on the threshold of freedom, like a soldier who, standing up in the trenches to announce the end of the war, had his head blown off by a bullet.

He was the last to die in Block 2. He drank the chalice to the dregs and was our last ghost.

And we waited…

We went on living, caught between the nascent hope of our likely release and the terror of its being an illusion.

The guards were confident, elated even. They'd become our friends. We were brothers in Islam now. Isn't forgiveness one of Islam's great virtues?

"If you have sinned towards us," they said, "we forgive you! And if we have sinned towards you, forgive us!"

After all, we were all soldiers, weren't we? We knew the meaning of service, orders and the rest of it. We could have been in their shoes. Of course we could… To one jailer who kept repeating this to me, I replied, "Do you know, even if this were to go on until the end of time, I would never swap places with you, not for all the treasure in the world."

The waiting, the uncertainty and even the hope were inhumane after so many years, so many ordeals and the cruelty of time, which stretches to infinity, swelling to shatter the patience of the wisest men.

We were only seven now in the building: the veterans (Skiba, Daoudi and me), the Bourriquat brothers and Achour, who had taken a rest cure in Block I for several months. The atmosphere was morose and speculation was rife, until that morning when the sparrows announced the guards, who opened everyone's cells except for the Bourriquats'. They ordered us to pick up what we had. There was general astonishment; we'd heard no vehicles and there'd been no activity that might have signalled pending release.

"You're going to the other block," they said sententiously.

This was a half measure, but it augured well.

I was incapable of thought. My mind was addled. They could have been taking us to hell and I'd have followed without a second thought.

When I reached the door, I stopped, blinded by the light, dazzled by the colour of the sky, bombarded by the smells of nature. I stopped, feeling the sun's intoxicating caress on my skin as my dazed memory tried desperately to find the proper places for these sensations in my consciousness.

The guards were patient, suddenly understanding. They let me have that moment, rare in any lifetime: to be born as an old man. The strange feeling a baby must have as it leaves its mother's belly, arriving in the world, but without a cry.

We walked on, stumbling under the weight of our belongings, our fears and our hopes. Our heightened senses took great greedy gulps of life, as if fearing it would run out. Since he knew the way, Achour broke into a run and rushed towards Block I. He had other concerns: to find the best place, as near as possible to the most privileged prisoner.

Our comrades were waiting for us, curious, excited and impatient. Some of them hadn't seen us in eighteen years, others – the pilots – had never seen us.

The encounter was charged with emotion; we'd left each other as young men and were returning as old men. Aziz Daoudi, Bouchaïb Skiba and I were in a very bad way. I could see just how bad in our hosts' astonished eyes. Some of them wept profusely. Everyone made a fuss of us. One offered vitamin tablets, another a bit of soap. They gave us shards of mirror, some rags, a whole array of small attentions. We'd fantasised so much about fate's favouring of this block, but they were shivering wrecks like us – a little better preserved perhaps, but just as ravaged, just as ruined.

We were leaving behind the Bourriquat brothers, with all the worry and anguish that that entailed. Questions, too: what would become of them? Why had they been separated from us? Would they be freed? What fate lay in store for them? They were an integral part of our group, just like the African stranger or Miloudi Seddiq. In Tazmamart, there were no pilots or infantry, civilians or military, officers or NCOs, black or white, Muslim or Christian; there were just men united by the same suffering, the same misery, and the unspeakable horror of our fall from grace.

The rumours became more precise: the end of the tunnel was in sight. Very quickly the mood lightened. I was in the cell next to Merzouki, who'd been in my year at the academy and was a friend. I was reunited, too, with my friends Chaoui and Rijali. The guards left the cell doors open, clearly having been given orders to do so. The meals improved, but nothing yet indicated a definite outcome. A change of plan was always possible.

I was torn. I couldn't bring myself to imagine the future. On the eve of momentous events, people usually surmise, imagine, hope. I could not. I clung to the present the way someone who's been shipwrecked clings to his saviour. Was this common sense or terror? I had no idea. I adopted the pragmatism of 'wait and see'. It avoided so many questions and would spare me great disappointment in the end.

As was their habit, the guards surprised us. In the middle of an afternoon in the first week of September 1991 they arrived, with no warning from the sparrows. They opened the doors to the block and told us to go back to our cells. Calling for silence, they ordered us to give back our things. This was a shock, though it was a lot less dramatic than in previous years: we weren't going to give up our skin but be given a new one.

I gave back what was left of my blankets and my rags with a pang: I felt apprehension, doubt and something like nostalgia, as in the moment of silence that follows a song, when the emotion still lingers in the soul.

Before the day was over, we were standing in our empty cells just as we had on the first day, but without our health, our youth or our innocence.

At dusk, trucks arrived. From inside, we could hear only curt orders flying above the engines' hum. There was no rush or confusion, which was unusual and indicated the presence of a high-ranking officer, no doubt the bloodthirsty Colonel Fadoul.

The guards entered the cells and had us leave one by one. Two uniformed gendarmes in fatigues awaited us in the corridor to cuff our hands behind our backs and put on the inevitable blindfolds. Two others took us by the shoulders and led us towards the vehicles. It was the choreography of horror, orchestrated by vampires in combat uniform.

When my turn arrived, I said to the gendarme holding the handcuffs, "I can't travel with my hands behind my back."

He looked at me in surprise and hesitated for a moment. He could see I was bent double, incapable of standing. His fellow soldier, who must have caught a sign or a glance from a superior, told him, "That's OK, put his hands in front of him."

I was glad of this small victory, but I didn't know what awaited me, what awaited us.

Wedged between two fellow prisoners on the truck's metal bench, my back against a grille of iron bars, I began the hardest, longest night of my life. As soon as the truck moved off, the torture began. I didn't have muscles or clothes to protect my decalcified bones from the nervous jolts of this mechanical beast. Thrown about at the mercy of the potholes on the secondary roads we followed, my skeleton caused me agonising pain. Every tremor reverberated through my whole being, along taut nerves that were ready to snap. I couldn't cry or even moan.

I was in a bone-grinding machine. It was a glimpse of hell, a continuous, incessant onslaught of piercing and relentless pain. My brain was paralysed, my thoughts scrambled. Never had my hope been so battered.

I prayed and suffered, stifled my sobs and suffered, panicked and suffered. I knew that nothing would stop this infernal machine except arrival at its destination.

The trek lasted a whole night and ended where it had all begun: in Ahermoumou, transformed for the occasion into a prison infirmary. The wheel had come full circle.

The trucks stopped. It was daylight already. The weather was mild and, above all, we were stationary at last. Now we could savour the fullness of this moment, the way torture victims savour moments of respite while their tormentor takes a break.

Solid arms held me up and walked me out of the truck. I could not stand or move unaided. One of the guards slipped his forearm beneath my armpit and dragged me towards my new lodgings. We were slow; I hadn't yet recovered from the pain and emotions of the night. After an obstacle course of corridors and escalators, we arrived. The gendarme removed my handcuffs and warned me that we were going through a doorway. He led me inside.

"Watch out," he said, "you're about to sit down on a bed."

Then he let go. I could already feel the mattress against my thighs when suddenly I fell into emptiness. My insides rose into my abdomen and my heart almost stopped, like a parachutist jumping from the plane for the first time. At last the fall ended and I began to rise to the surface again. The guard removed my blindfold and I found myself in a big, well-lit, clean, white room. I was on a bed, a real bed, with a sprung base, so soft I'd thought I was falling into nothingness.

When the guards left I stayed in my palace, broken and exhausted but with all my senses on high alert. I drank my fill of light, sucked up the oxygen, luxuriated in the cleanness, rolled around in my bed, wondered at the toilet with its immaculate sink and seat, and then those big windows, with no bars.

The meal was just as good: fried steak with a little sauce, mashed potato, a crusty baguette, an apple and a yoghurt. It wasn't haute cuisine, but at that moment nothing could have tasted better. We were allowed a hot shower with soap; although brief, it was more beneficial than all the different medicines we were given. I felt renewed, as if all the years of horror, grief and tears had been washed away. There was a whole flurry of doctors with different areas of expertise, who weren't there to treat us but to patch us up and make us presentable to the world on our release; to keep up appearances in a world, in a country, where appearances were everything.

We were allowed to see a dentist, too; we'd lost most of our teeth, some of us had lost all of them. This was an opportunity to leave my room. The dentist's surgery was in a lorry parked in front of the building we were in, in the middle of a little square overlooking the vast cliff by the school.

To conceal the landscape and stop us from recognising where we were – but also to deter prying eyes from the outside world – civilian and military vehicles had been parked around the square. For the first time since my arrest, I went outside without handcuffs or a blindfold. The emotion that hit me was overpowering: in the background, snow-capped Bou Iblan in the harsh summer sun seemed to emerge from the vast emptiness that was palpable behind the barrier of futuristic-looking trucks and cars. I thought I was looking at spacecraft; for a moment I thought I was on another planet. But soon I returned to reality when I saw the armed gendarmes looking at me curiously, as if at an exotic animal or the remains of a prehistoric man.

I went into the surgery, which was bathed in light. It was immaculately clean and well organised. The dentist glowed just as brightly as his vehicle. I was fascinated by his manicured fingers, his nails cut short, his almost translucent, clean-smelling skin. He spoke, I didn't hear him. My overloaded senses were concentrated in my eyes, into which all this life was gushing. Hands took hold of me delicately and lifted me up. Ah, it was over. I stood up automatically and time suddenly stopped. Around me, everything froze: I was looking into a mirror, rapt, hypnotised by this gaze from beyond, those wild eyes that looked me up and down. Whose were they? Where did they come from? For a moment I thought of Van Gogh's gaze. No, no, this wasn't madness; it was something else, something far beyond that. I prised myself away from those eyes to stare at the face of an old man that I had trouble recognising or accepting. It was me.

I went back to my room, unable to rid myself of the vision of the half-mad ascetic I'd seen in the mirror. His gaze would follow me for years to come, and still today I don't know if I've seen the last of him.

During this transition period, it was enough to look and to listen. I refused to enter into any discussions with anyone in charge who wanted to salve their conscience with an ostensibly caring gesture or, more cynically, a condescending one. I would simply look them straight in the eye and not reply. That made them uncomfortable, but I didn't give a damn for their pity.

The fateful day arrived. It was already a week since our best-preserved comrades had been released. Knowing the press would be waiting for us outside, the authorities had decided to free us in small groups, starting with the most presentable. When my turn arrived, Colonel Fadoul came to find me, accompanied by a doctor, and announced that the king, in his great leniency, had pardoned me and that I should be eternally grateful to him. In return, when I left, I should not talk to any journalists or make any public statements… Bowing my head, I listened religiously, humbly, submissively, the most obedient of his Gracious Majesty's subjects. I had just one thought in mind: under no circumstances would I relive the torture I'd suffered during our transfer from Tazmamart. When he finished, I blurted out, "Colonel, I won't be able to cope with the truck journey. I'd arrive in a very bad way. How would I be able to stand when I see my family and the people who come to see me?"

The argument was a strong one. He turned to the doctor and asked his opinion. The doctor agreed. They began to work out a solution. Time was running out. I was ready with my answer because I'd been thinking about it for two months. I looked at the doctor and suggested, "Could you put a mattress in the truck?"

The colonel shouted a name, whose owner appeared as if by magic, "Put his mattress in the truck for him!"

"Yes, Colonel!"

Fadoul the torturer had just spared me six hundred kilometres of further torture.

The journey passed as I'd imagined. I had two fellow soldiers with me who endured the torment of this mode of transport. Even though I was cuffed and blindfolded, I was by turns lying down or sitting on my mattress and, when I was dropped at the Gendarmes' General HQ in Marrakech, I was well rested.

A car took me to the administrative centre of the district where my mother lived. The area's security chiefs were there in force, in the caid's office. The caid used the same language as Colonel Fadoul, but there was no journey at stake now. I was content to stare silently into his eyes, not even blinking. He was embarrassed, squirming in his seat. I imagined him confronted with that half-crazed look that had shocked me so deeply. The chief superintendent, sensing his discomfort, came to his aid. "I think we ought to let this gentleman be with his family."

The caid took the hint and signalled to an aide who ushered two people into the room. I recognised my brother, Abdellah, but not my younger sister, Ilham, who'd been fifteen when I was arrested. As we left the office, I noticed a gendarme standing there. I took off the big military coat I was wearing and handed it to him.

"Here, take this," I said. "It belongs to you."

Acknowledgements

The author would like to thank my fairy godmother Lulu Norman who fought long and hard, then by waving her magic wand, to bring off this book in the language of Shakespeare, and to Haus Publishing for their trust and professionalism. All my thanks for everything.

The translator would like to thank Aziz BineBine, but words fail… His trust, generosity and patience, and that of Mahi Binebine and Amia Binebine, made this book possible. Thanks also to the incomparable Barnaby Rogerson, whose knowledge and passion helped it find a home, and to Ros Schwartz, whose skill and experience greatly benefited the text. Thanks to Rémi Labrusse and Alexander Norman, who read the book early and both contributed specialist knowledge. Thanks – always – to Isobel Boyt, Fran, Nick and Gene Jensen-Costelloe, for keeping me going, to my wonderful editor, Alice Horne, and to Barbara Schwepcke, Harry Hall and everyone at Haus Publishing.